CONNECTING TO MY
FUTURE

A Learning and Planning Guide
for Salon Professionals

paul mitchell the school publications

First published in the USA by Paul Mitchell Advanced Education LLC
and PAUL MITCHELL THE SCHOOL
1226 West South Jordan Parkway
Unit C-200
South Jordan, Utah 84095
(866) 302-5576

www.paulmitchelltheschool.com

First Published 2004
Copyright © 2004 Paul Mitchell Advanced Education LLC

ISBN# 0-9743205-0-1

Writer: Susan Papageorgio, Inspired Learning LLC.
Publishing Director: Susan Papageorgio, Inspired Learning LLC.
Editing: Martha Quirk
Graphic Design: Jane Lacy, JSL Design LLC.
Cover Artwork: Smith & Jones Design, Auben LS. Frith
Photography: Dazzo

Contents

THANK YOU THANK YOU
THANK YOU

The inspiring and brilliant ideas contained in this book are made possible because of the following people:

Consultation Team
Tommy Callahan
Kate Caussey
Dennis James
Monica Mathews
Tova Stroman
Audra Turner

Development Team
Marie Carter
Brennan Claybaugh
Jamie Griffin
Chris Halladay
Mike Helm
Kathy Hutching
Cindy S. Nielson
Carolyn Nelson
Lori Noble
Michelle Swendsen
Jodi Wonacott

Publication Team
Winn Claybaugh
Auben Frith
Mary Anne Gross
Jane Lacy
Susan Papageorgio
Martha Quirk
Molly Quirk
Suzanne Zipperer

Contributors

Neeko Abriol
Louis Atkins
Josh Banks
Michael Cole
Angie Cranor
Robert Cromeans
John Paul DeJoria
Jay Eklund
Susie Fields

Eric Fisher
Dennis James
Melissa Jaqua
Gene Juarez
Stephanie Kocielski
Jill Kohler
Sydell Miller
Mary Rector-Gable
Laini Reeves
Melissa Ryan
John Ryan

Sister Bonnie Steinlage
David Stanko
Kate Troc
David Wagner
William Williams

In Loving Memory of

Andrew Gomez

The John Paul Mitchell Systems' Story

Over 20 years ago, two friends had a vision—to establish a company by hairdressers for hairdressers—one that would provide tools of success for Future and Salon Professionals, their salons, and the entire beauty industry. It all began in 1979, when John Paul DeJoria and Paul Mitchell first decided to launch their professional hair care system around a revolutionary new styling method and a new styling product.

By 1980, they had established a partnership with a borrowed $750, which eventually became known as JOHN PAUL MITCHELL SYSTEMS®. The two partners began marketing their products under the brand name PAUL MITCHELL®, as Mr. Mitchell was the hairdresser of the two and other hairdressers would respect a hairdresser's name.

Initially, John Paul Mitchell Systems faced many challenges. According to Mr. DeJoria, "We should have gone bankrupt perhaps 50 times during the first year." Resources were so limited that the PAUL MITCHELL® brand's now famous black and white packaging was a result of not being able to afford colored ink. At one point, the company consisted of a post office box and an answering machine featuring the voice of a female friend (with an English accent) to convey that there was, indeed, an "office."

The partners Mitchell and DeJoria traveled extensively to conduct no-cost product demonstrations for salon owners and guaranteed salon owners that they would sell all products purchased; if they didn't, they could return any unsold products for a full refund. Their commitment led to John Paul Mitchell Systems becoming one of the fastest growing privately held companies in the United States. Tragically, Paul Mitchell died of pancreatic cancer in 1989.

The two partners' dream has flourished. Today, John Paul Mitchell Systems is a multimillion dollar company, and John Paul continues to steer it according to the original vision. The privately held company is committed to the success of the salons and Salon Professionals who have offered support throughout the years.

John Paul Mitchell Systems' products, which include the brand names PAUL MITCHELL®, Modern Elixirs™, The Tea Tree Collection™, and JPMS The Color™, are manufactured exclusively in the United States. Products are sold through 25 distributors within the United States to approximately 90,000 hair salons. Internationally, John Paul Mitchell Systems works with distributors in 45 countries that supply thousands of hair salons.

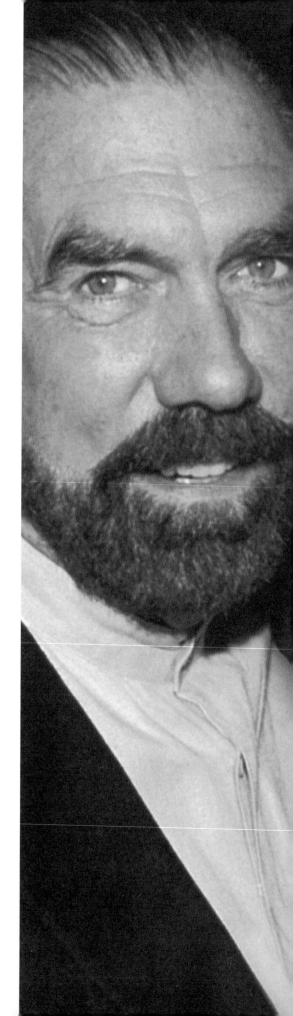

"Connect with
your future
by being in the
present moment
and keeping your
vision focused on
the things that bring
you the most joy.
This is the path
of a visionary."

PAUL MITCHELL THE SCHOOL

Welcome

We are happy you decided to join our industry. Get ready to learn, laugh, and have fun. You have chosen one of the best industries in the world. This book was written to show you all that you can be when you follow your dream and take action. You are the future educators, business owners, product manufacturers, industry organization presidents, and successful professionals. Allow us to help you achieve more than you can imagine at this moment. Allow us to help you to connect with your future, starting now!

Why was *Connecting To My Future* written? *Connecting To My Future* is a guide that is inspired by John Paul and the many other visionaries who have created and contributed to the beauty industry. Within each chapter you will learn from the experience and brilliance of others who have passionately followed their dreams and welcome you to join them on the path to success.

Our Gift to You

This book is dedicated to you, Future Professionals and new professionals, who have a dream and vision to create success and happiness within your life.

This guide is to show you the path to success, to provide guidance when you are not sure what to do, and to help you create professional and personal happiness.

Vision forward

Learn about:

John Paul DeJoria

- Chairman and Chief Executive Officer of John Paul Mitchell Systems.

- Co-Founder of PAUL MITCHELL THE SCHOOL.

- Entrepreneur, business owner, father, husband, and mentor.

- Student told by his high school teacher that he would "never, ever succeed at anything in life," John Paul set out to prove him wrong!

Learn from:

- John Paul DeJoria

- Winn Claybaugh

DEAR SALON PROFESSIONAL:

I want to take this opportunity to welcome you to the most amazing industry on the planet! The professional beauty industry encompasses some of the most passionate, caring, and FUN human beings on the planet.

Many years ago, I had the opportunity of connecting with one such industry professional, Mr. Winn Claybaugh. Winn is a man who has inspired and motivated thousands upon thousands of Salon Professionals worldwide. But he has another talent, the ability to create a learning environment that has produced some of the most motivated, talented, and successful hairdressers I have ever met.

I knew that Winn and his team had a magic formula the first time I visited Von Curtis Academy in Provo, Utah. The energy was overwhelming; it was more like walking into a busy, upscale, successful salon than into a beauty school. We have now joined forces, and I am extremely proud to be partnered with Winn and his team in PAUL MITCHELL THE SCHOOL.

The underlying philosophy is really a simple one: set yourself up to win. Passing the state board and getting licensed is just one step in the process of being a true professional. This learning and planning guide is an example of how much more there is to being truly successful. I am extremely proud that PAUL MITCHELL THE SCHOOL provides a unique learning environment to nurture and educate career-minded superprofessionals who create great hair, gain hair show experience, build merchandising and promotional skills, and acquire the information required to be a great business person.

I urge each and every one of you to take advantage of the opportunities set before you. Take it all in, and apply it in your own way, in your own lives. The keys to success are here and yours for the taking! Enjoy, live, learn, and laugh!

John Paul DeJoria
Chairman and Chief Executive Officer
John Paul Mitchell Systems

WINN CLAYBAUGH

Winn Claybaugh is the co-founder of PAUL MITCHELL THE SCHOOL and is a nationally recognized motivation expert and speaker.

Winn co-hosts a monthly audio magazine called MASTERS and has been a featured emcee of the North American Hairdressing Awards among his accomplishments.

Winn loves to sing and play the piano. He used his concert grand piano to fund the first education event and is called a "mover of mountains" by American Salon Magazine. Winn is the former vice president of the AIDS Relief Fund for Beauty Professionals, with board members Whoopi Goldberg, Cher, Vidal Sassoon, and John Paul DeJoria. Winn has also interviewed Larry King.

Good habits bring good fortune and success, while bad habits ultimately block success. A habit is something you do all of the time, which may become embedded in your behavior. Seemingly unimportant, harmless daily activities can, over time, transform into destructive patterns that can hold you back.

In this guide we are going to challenge you to reflect on, change, and develop positive patterns that will ultimately bring you success.

We will ask you to fine-tune your thinking, dressing, hygiene, learning, communication, client service, goal-setting, and organizational habits. Your habits are the bite-size steps you can change in order to "play big." What will happen if you decided not to change your habits and learn from others who have gone before you? That's simple. You will learn through experiencing pain, "bad luck," and missed opportunities. This is known as the "school of hard knocks." This path of learning is also effective, but it simply takes longer. By reading and applying the concepts in this book, you will learn to play big a lot faster, and you will have more fun doing it. You will discover that you can learn through play rather than pain.

> "Good habits bring good fortune and success, while bad habits ultimately block success."

Join others before you who have learned to have fun, playing big in an industry that is full of learning opportunities. Choose to learn from the experiences of others. Apply their wisdom to what you currently are doing and you will make your own "luck."

"Make your own 'luck.'"

Winn Claybaugh

"If you want to
be successful,
look around to see
what everyone else
is doing and do
something different."

*Walt Disney, American animator
and film producer*

Introduction

In this segment get the big picture. Create a road map called a *game plan* and meet the mentors or the people you can learn from who are featured in each chapter.

Create a Road Map for Your Journey

Game planning begins by looking at the big picture. It's important before you start on any journey to have a road map that outlines your route. Take a moment before you dive into this guide to look at the big picture of what this book has to offer. During this introductory segment, we will recommend that you take time to preview or take a tour of this guide by scanning through each chapter, which will help you to uncover the areas you would like to develop and ways you would like to grow.

During the introduction, we will ask you to create your game plan for success. You will return to your game plan throughout your learning while reading this book. You will set goals, identify key questions, and create a list of commitments that will help you to put your ideas into action. Your game plan will help you to gain perspective on how to get the most out of your reading.

Tips for Success

This guide is designed to be an interactive learning tool that you may use to develop successful habits. You may want to read the entire book and then do the activities within each chapter, or you may want to take several months to explore the information and to "try on" the suggestions within each segment. We don't ask you to "buy" everything in the book, we are simply asking you to "try it on" as if you were trying on a beautiful outfit before you buy it. If it works, then buy it; if it doesn't, then put it back for a while.

Each person has a unique approach to learning. We recommend that you simply find your preferred way to learn from lessons offered in this book. You have already taken the first step to success; you bought or received this guide and you are reading it. Now take time to apply what you learn to make your life better.

See the big picture

Think about:

- What is good luck?

- Who can I learn from?

- What tips for learning may I apply during the process?

- What is my game plan for success?

- What does it mean to "try it on"?

Learn about:

- The big picture.

- Your game plan.

The Big Picture, Connecting To My Future

Connecting To My Future will help you to transform yourself into your new role, which is a successful, confident, knowledgeable Salon Professional. *Connecting To My Future* is a fun guide that will help you to develop and organize yourself so that you may achieve your dreams and goals.

Are You Ready to Connect with Your Future Now?
To start your learning process, take a moment to flip through the entire book. You will notice that each chapter is a "learning journey" designed to help you develop a specific aspect of yourself. This guide features many wonderful ideas and experiences from successful people throughout the industry. Take time to read their stories and apply their advice. Your new learning path is outlined within chapters of this guide. The road map to connect with your future includes:

My Outlook
Your thoughts, beliefs, and actions are what create your experiences, and ultimately, your success. Focus on what will bring you happiness, success, and joy.

My Brain
How can you make your learning easy and fun? How can you remember what you learned and implement new skills? You will discover that effective learning is a simple skill that you can develop to gain success in every area of your life.

My Style
Learn how to fine-tune your personal image for success. If you want to "play big," you have to look and feel like a successful professional, which will help you to attract and connect with clients.

My Gear

You are a craftsperson who must use tools to successfully perform your craft and develop your business. Learn about the essential tools of your trade. Learn about how to get them, create them, and care for them.

My Clients

Business is like theater. Your place of work is your stage; you play a specific role with a script, while your clients are your audience. Learn to create a service environment and experience that clients love.

My Mentors

There are many people around you who want you to succeed and are willing to help you. These people can become your mentors. Work smarter, not harder. Find and work with mentors who will broaden your perspective.

My Future

Learn about the industry you are entering. The beauty industry does not just exist in the four walls of your school or salon; it exists in the activities within the professional community. Join and connect with school activities, salon businesses, and industry events. Become an active part of the industry now.

My Plan

Identify and commit to a game plan that will help you to focus your thoughts and actions toward your ultimate goal. Identify your new role and job description. Create a career path of your dreams. Each precious moment is an opportunity to succeed, grow, learn, and have fun.

> *Each precious moment is an opportunity to succeed, grow, learn, and have fun."*

Connecting Tip   #1

Live, Laugh, Learn

To become a "superprofessional" choose a professional environment that is fun, nurturing, and provides opportunities to develop your technical, fashion, and promotional skills. Focus on learning and enjoying what you do.

Connect with Your Mentors

Connecting To My Future includes ideas and suggestions from people around the industry. Read their remarkable stories. Learn from their wisdom. They will inspire you.

John Paul DeJoria

Winn Claybaugh

Chapter 1
Angie Cranor

Chapter 1
Neeko Abriol

Chapter 1
David Wagner

Chapter 2
Dennis James

Chapter 3
Stephanie Kocielski

Chapter 3
Melissa Jaqua

Chapter 3
Jay Eklund

Chapter 4
David Stanko

Chapter 4
Laini Reeves

Chapter 5
Melissa Ryan

Chapter 5
John Ryan

Chapter 5
Kate Troc

Chapter 6
Robert Cromeans

Chapter 6
Sister Bonnie Steinlage

Chapter 7
Mary Rector-Gable

Chapter 8
Josh Banks

Chapter 8
Susie Fields

Chapter 8
Michael Cole

Tips for Learning in This Guide:

 This guide is designed to help you to learn and grow. The following are tips that will help you to have fun and get the most out of your learning experience. Enjoy your reading.

Start with your interests — Start in the areas that are most interesting to you. There is no need to start from the beginning and read each chapter. Learning can be fun and easy when you focus on what you are interested in.

Put your learning into action — The best way to learn is to put what you have read into action. Within each chapter you will notice that there are learning activities that will help you to remember and apply the wisdom of the mentors and experts within that specific area. Immediately practicing and applying what you are learning is very important to improving and retaining what you have learned.

Connect daily — You will notice we have placed **Connecting Tip** cards throughout the book. Refer to them each day. Try on the new ideas and apply them to your life. You will be amazed at the results.

Have fun — Make your learning fun. Work on your "learning journeys," the learning within each chapter, only when you are in the mood and focused. Choose to "try on" and play with what you have learned.

Make discoveries — During your learning process you may discover that some of the things you try will work and others may not work on your first try. Consider your "mistakes" to be *discoveries.* Be willing to step away from what has always made you comfortable, take a risk, and stretch yourself. Your path to connecting to your future is a journey filled with discoveries, not failures.

Two heads are better than one — Try working with a "learning partner." Working with someone else will make your learning more fun, interesting, and social. You and your partner can challenge each other and make learning easier.

Show what you know — Finally, share this book with others who you know: your team members, your teachers, your family, your friends, and even your children. The concepts within this guide are universal and can be applied to almost any person in your life. Teaching others what you have learned is the best form of learning.

Create your game plan — The key to having fun and making learning easy is to recognize that you are already very smart. You already have knowledge and experience that you can draw upon. You now need a plan to expand upon your experience and develop new skills. The steps to creating a successful game plan include:

- Identifying what you would like to learn first and the key questions you may have about the topic. You will find thought-provoking questions at the beginning of each chapter. Take time to read through these questions.

- Identifying what thoughts or fears you may have that may block you from meeting your learning goals.

- Creating learning goals that help you to learn. As you read each chapter, determine what you want to learn and apply to your life.

- Making commitments and following through to change your behavior and habits. Your follow-through is the most important thing you can do to succeed.

Interests and questions — Remember to always start with *F.U.N.* (fun)! As you page through the book, what chapters or topics look the most interesting to you? Identify areas within this book that are most interesting to you. List them below. Next, identify at least one question you would like to answer about that topic. As you read and learn, remember you may get questions from the beginning of each chapter.

What topics interest me?

Questions I most want to answer:

1. _____

2. _____

3. _____

4. _____

5. _____

Learning blocks — Each of us has had many learning experiences. By the age of 18, you have experienced approximately 14,000 hours of classroom learning. You are already an experienced learner. Some of your experiences may have been positive, while others may have been uncomfortable, boring, or even painful. You experience a learning block when you close yourself off to learning or trying new things because of past unpleasant experiences.

Your learning blocks may be your beliefs, fears, distractions, or any bad habits that keep you from growing and changing. Take a moment and think about how you have learned in the past. What were some of the things that have kept you from learning? For example, many people are afraid of making mistakes, being embarrassed, or being criticized, so they never risk breaking out of their comfort zone. Think about the little voice inside that may hold you back from learning and changing. Check the one that whispers: "I don't have time," "That looks dumb," "How boring," or "I can't do that!" This voice will keep you from learning and growing.

There may have been a time when you struggled to learn something new. You may not have gotten the help you needed, or you may have felt embarrassed because others were able to "get it" and you didn't. A learning block for you may be that when you are learning you are afraid you won't understand.

Another learning block example may be an experience from the past when a teacher inadvertently or purposely embarrassed you after you made a mistake. A block you may now have is that you are afraid of making mistakes. The best way to handle fear is to identify it, let it go, and redirect your thinking.

Distractions are another example of learning blocks. You may become easily distracted with activities that take you away from your goals. For example, watching too much television is a distraction and a habit that may keep you from focusing on other things. What personal habits could you let go of to make room for new interests and pursuits?

Let go of learning blocks!
Identify the things you need to let go of: your beliefs, fears, and habits that will take you away from your learning. Ask yourself, "What would keep me from learning from this book?" Write your learning blocks below:

1. _____

2. _____

3. _____

4. _____

5. _____

Create a confidence statement — Now see yourself in the future. Pretend that you have already completed this book and have completed your learning. Imagine that you have applied the key concepts and you are now know-ledgeable, skilled, and successful. Imagine what a sense of accomplishment you would feel. Now think of a statement that you could use to help you focus on what you want to accomplish and redirect your thoughts away from anything that may block you. This is called a *confidence statement* or an *affirmation*. Remember your confidence statement and say it when you are feeling blocked or unsure.

> *"Remember your confidence statement and say it when you are feeling blocked or unsure."*

My confidence statement:

_____

_____

Some examples are: "My success is guaranteed," "I am a talented hairdresser," and "I love to learn."

You will use this statement over and over as you are learning from this guide. Create a statement that reflects what you would like to accomplish, put it on a 3 x 5-inch card, and post it where you will read it often.

Create goals and commitment — Throughout this guide, you will be asked to complete several activities that will help you to discover new information, learn steps to improve your performance, and finally create a commitment to change. The most critical time of your game plan is when you make commitments or promises to yourself. The most powerful thing you can do is to follow through. Think of a time when a friend promised to do something important for you and did not follow through. How did you feel? You may have felt disappointed or that you couldn't count on the friend. So love yourself enough to follow through on the promises you make, especially to yourself.

Promises, promises! — What's interesting is that we all make promises and commitments to ourselves, and many times we don't follow through. We dismiss it with excuses like: "I was too busy," or "I couldn't follow through because of my boss or my instructor," or "It doesn't matter, I didn't really want to do that!" These excuses are what keep us from getting what we really want.

Start now — Make a commitment to follow through, to truly push yourself to learn and grow. Make promises to yourself that you will keep. See yourself as if you had already completed your lessons and have obtained your goals. Stay focused on what you want and don't give up until you achieve it.

Make a commitment — Think of a commitment you could make right now that will help you to achieve what you want and write it on your commitment list on Page 19.

For example, you may want to promise yourself that you will read a chapter of this guide each week. Or that you will discuss what you have learned with a learning partner or friend. You will be asked to make additional commitments as you read each chapter. Finally, a very important commitment you will want to make is that you will read this book with an open mind.

You will discover that when you embrace your successes, let go of your fears, identify your goals, and make commitments to change that you will become the master of your future. Your vision will expand, you will experience more confidence, and you will have a map for success called your *game plan.*

Connecting Tip   #2

Practice Big. Play Big.

Your success depends on how well you practice.
Practice "playing big" by adopting successful habits.

If you develop good habits and practice like those
who are successful, eventually you will "play big."

Source: Papageorgio, Susan. Game Planning curriculum. Inspired Learning LLC, 1997.

My Commitments

As you read through the book you will want to return to this page to mark down your ideas and commitments.

My focus:	I will get there by:	I will complete it by:
I will read this guide with an open mind.	I will meet with (list name) each week to discuss and apply concepts I have read.	I will complete this guide in 8 weeks on (list date). I will meet with my mentor each Tuesday at 7 a.m.
WHAT I WILL FOCUS ON:	**STEPS I WILL TAKE:**	**WHEN I WILL DO IT:**
Chapter 1		
Chapter 2		
Chapter 3		
Chapter 4		
Chapter 5		
Chapter 6		
Chapter 7		
Chapter 8		

"Do or do not.
There is no try!"

Yoda, Star Wars *sage*

BELIE

Chapter 1

My Outlook

How do your beliefs affect your life? In this chapter we are going to take a journey into your mind to explore your mental "programming." You will examine some of the core beliefs you have about yourself.

You will discover that what you focus on creates your experiences. You will also learn how to make simple changes in your habits to create more fun, success, and happiness in your personal and professional life.

Finally, we are going to look at examples of other really cool people who have "been there, done that." You will love their stories of how they took control of their thoughts, emotions, and mental habits to create their current success.

Explore your thoughts and beliefs to create success

Think about:

- What do I focus on?

- What do I regularly think about?

- What do I say about myself?

- How do I hold myself back from achieving?

- Do my friends consider me a positive or a negative person?

- How can I create joy, peace, and success?

Learn about:

- Control your programming.
- Choose your focus.
- Love what you do.
- Be nice.

Learn from:

- Angie Cranor
- Neeko Abriol
- David Wagner

Your Programming

Think of how a computer works. It is programmed to run specific functions and tasks. The computer's software determines the type of output it provides. The software relies on information that is put into it. When the computer receives input that is accurate, it performs well. In contrast, when the computer receives inaccurate or "garbage" information, it gives unusable garbage back. This is known as "garbage in and garbage out" or *G.I.G.O.*

Your mind is similar to computer software. The quality of the information you allow into your brain directly affects your thinking, beliefs, and behavior. What happens when you feed your mind garbage by focusing on negative things? What happens when you surround yourself with negative people? How do you feel when you focus on violence, gossip, or meanness? Do you worry or perhaps become irritated and tired? You may find that what you focus on can affect your mood.

On the flip side, what happens when you focus on the positive and productive things in your life? Do you feel motivated, optimistic, and more energetic? Would you agree with the following statements?

- What I focus on is really up to me.

- I have control over my thoughts.

- When I focus on things that are distracting or negative, my beliefs change and my behavior is affected.

These statements are the starting points to taking control of your life. There are five steps that may help you to change your outlook and your life.

Five steps to taking control of your life

Step 1:   Cancel the negative.

Step 2:   Choose your focus.

Step 3:   Manage your self-talk.

Step 4:   Choose love.

Step 5:   Be nice.

STEP 1 Cancel the Negative, Choose the Positive

Think about people you know who have more bad days than good days. Bad things always seem to happen to them. They may get sick a lot. They tend to have "bad luck." They rarely have good things to say and love talking about the negative drama happening around them. They begin conversations with, "You think *you* had a bad day. Wait until you hear what happened to me." They focus on drama after drama. Dramatic people may give great haircuts, but they de-energize their clients in the process.

 Such people tend to be pessimistic and sarcastic. Things they have no control over, such as the weather or traffic, can make them miserable. They love to complain and criticize. They see a glass of water filled to the midpoint as "half empty."

Now think about people you know who are generally happy. They love to try new things. They are almost always in a good mood. They tend to be lucky. They are usually complimentary about others. They are open, flexible, and optimistic. Such people see the same glass of water as "half full."

The person who sees the glass half full tends to focus on the positive and productive. They program themselves to allow positive influences to affect their thinking and avoid negative influences. Are you the half-empty type or the half-full type? Does your presence actually inspire people or poison and upset them?

How It Works

As adults we all have control over the programming we put into our minds. We choose what to watch on TV, what movies to see, and what conversations to pay attention to. All those sources are part of our programming. Your programming influences your thoughts. Your thoughts become actions. Actions become habits, and habits form your character and your personality. It's that simple.

You think you *had a bad day."*

Dramatic people may give great haircuts, but they can de-energize their clients."

If your preferred programming is watching negative soap operas, then your life will become a negative soap opera with you in the starring role.

What would be the benefit of taking control of where you focus? You can choose your programming and cut the drama out of your life. You can decide to be miserable or happy. It's your choice. Start by taking an inventory of what you spend your time focusing on.

If it bleeds, it leads."

Sources of Garbage

 Think of the following as common things that may be negatively influencing your thinking:

First 10 minutes of a newscast — The most negative and violent news always leads each newscast. Newscasters know they can hook you with the drama. They say, "If it bleeds, it leads." The first half of the newscast focuses on the bad news, while the last half focuses on human interest stories.

Talk shows — Talk shows tend to focus on gossip and negative behavior. They feature the most critical, tragic, and petty side of human nature.

Violent themes — Violence has become commonplace in movies, videos, music, TV programs, and books. People who focus on violence become desensitized to it.

Negative or degrading story themes — Story lines that are degrading to groups of people or have a negative premise tend to depress your thoughts and affect your emotions.

Gossip is unattractive."

Gossip — The dictionary defines *gossip* as "mischievous talk about someone else's affairs." Have you ever felt the sting of someone gossiping about you? Have you noticed how unattractive others look when they gossip? Gossip is unattractive. You are in a business to make others beautiful, and gossip does the opposite.

How much time do you spend negatively programming your brain?

How many hours per week do you read disturbing
stories in the newspaper?   _____

How much time do you spend listening to gruesome stories
that dominate news broadcasts?   _____

How many hours per week do you spend watching soap operas,
negative reality shows, talk shows, or shows that degrade others?   _____

How many hours per week do you go to movies with negative themes?   _____
*(Average the total minutes of negative or violent movies you see; for example,
one two-hour movie per month equals 30 minutes per week).*

How many hours per week do you listen to or engage
in gossip or negative conversation with others?   _____

Total hours focusing on "garbage" per week.   Total _____

Now multiply your total garbage hours by 100.   x 100 = _____

Why multiply your total hours of garbage programming
by 100? For each hour you have spent focusing on negative
programming or "garbage," you need a minimum of 100
hours of positive programming to counteract the effects.
If you watch a negative, violent movie for two hours, you
need 200 hours of positive programming to create
happiness and success.

Negative programming is very powerful. It subtly and
drastically shapes your thoughts. Don't fool yourself into
thinking that garbage programming won't somehow affect
your professional career.

The most effective approach to changing your brain's
programming is to minimize the amount of time you spend
focusing on things that create negativity in your life. When
confronted by negativity, ask yourself, "Do I have that much
time to reprogram?" Eliminate negativity. Get rid of it. Take
the garbage out!

Create a New Program to Make Your Heart Sing

Start by focusing on what makes your heart sing. Choose to spend time doing things that contribute to you as a person. Broaden your thought process. Focus on being informed. Discover ways to uplift your spirit.

Think about the things that you would consider positive programming. What television programs could you watch? What books could you read? What audio tapes could you listen to? What activities contribute to your well-being? Create a list of uplifting things you may do to change your perspective, and post it where you will see it often.

Things that make me happy

Watching inspirational movies and TV shows

Exercising or playing sports

Enjoying fresh flowers

Eating healthy, nutritious foods

Listening to my favorite music

Driving a clean car

Talking and visiting with family, friends, or mentors

Enjoying a clean, organized living space

STEP 2 Choose Your Focus

The next step is to choose your focus. Imagine driving a car. You are riding on a road called "your life." The road you are driving on represents all of the experiences and opportunities coming your way. As you drive you notice all of the wonderful things going on around you. You notice all of the opportunities and options available to you. You are focused on where you currently are and where you are going. You are happy because you are focused on the things you can change.

Now there's one more thing you could focus on—your rearview mirror. It represents the past. It could represent where you have been, including your past mistakes and old beliefs. What would happen if you drove down the road focusing only on your rearview mirror? You could get lost or even crash. You would be unhappy because you are focused on things you cannot change.

You may also notice that during the times you focus on your rearview mirror, you tend to worry about the future. This is because your focus carries the negative experiences from your past into your present. It is okay to glance back once in a while to learn from your past, but your main focus should always be the present and future. Worrying depletes energy and distracts you from your focus.

Your New Focus List

Here are some simple suggestions to help you focus on the present rather than the past.

- **Don't worry, be happy** — Worrying is a form of negative goal-setting. Focusing on what you don't want to happen can actually draw that reality to you. Your thoughts are instructions for your computer-like mind and your mind follows every instruction you give it, whether positive or negative.

- **Focus on the present and the positive** — In contrast, if you focus on the present, you become much more open to solutions. When you focus on the positive, you have better control of your emotions and your actions.

- **Minimize the time you focus on your problems** — Focusing on what you hate about a situation will only make you miserable. When you focus on your problems, you can't see the solutions.

- **Replace excuses with action** — If you're good at coming up with excuses, you will never be good at anything else. Instead of making excuses, take action. When you take action to make things better, you feel energized and empowered.

- **See problems as challenges that have solutions** — Whenever you experience a challenging situation, redirect your thoughts away from all of the drama and to the solutions by asking questions like:

  Where are my opportunities?

  What can I do to make this situation better?

  What steps can I take to make improvements?

  What am I learning?

If you are good at coming up with excuses, you will never be good at anything else."

- **Make a commitment** — Once you have identified what you would like to change, write down your plan and post it where you will see it often. Then follow through.

- **Practice daily** — Transformational changes do not happen overnight. You don't go to the gym one time and think that's all you need to be in shape. Make small adjustments every day until you achieve the change you want. Take the "crawl, walk, run" approach to making changes.

- **Be consistent** — Apply these tools consistently in all aspects of your life. Each time you encounter a challenge, quickly recognize where you are. Shift your focus to solutions, and then take action.

"You can experience tremendous change simply by envisioning yourself already achieving what you want and then talking 'as if' it has already happened."

STEP **3** Manage Your Self-Talk

One of the best ways to change your focus is to change the way you talk to yourself and about yourself, which is called *self-talk*. A great way to test your self-talk is to look in the mirror while you are wearing a bathing suit. What messages come to mind? Are you thinking, "I'm fat and out-of-shape," "If only my legs were longer," or "Why can't I have a better body?" Or think about what you say to yourself when you are learning something new. Do you say, "I'm not smart," "I'm a slow learner," "I'll fail," or "I don't want to be criticized."

You can experience tremendous change simply by envisioning yourself already achieving what you want and then talking "as if" it has already happened.

For example, imagine yourself already attaining your goals. You are vibrant, healthy, and full of energy. You are spending time with wonderful, positive friends. You have a loving relationship with your family. You are paying all of your bills on time and can afford the little luxuries. Visualize yourself truly happy and fulfilled. Now what would your self-talk be like?

The secret to happiness is to feel good about yourself first and to choose language that supports your thoughts. Your self-talk can greatly affect your thoughts and emotions.

ANGIE CRANOR

Angie Cranor is a graduate of Von Curtis Academy of Hair Design in Provo, Utah, and a successful stylist. She owns her own salon in spite of having to overcome many obstacles. An inspiring speaker who is familiar to many Salon Professionals, Angie truly lives her life as an example of what you can do if you just focus on what you want.

At age 16, I found my first true love—basketball. It was my life. I truly only felt like myself when I was on the court. I remember the game when my dad said, "Angie, play this game like it's the last game you'll ever play. Give it 100 percent." Well, I didn't take it to heart. I was only 16, and thought I would have the rest of my life to play ball.

The next day I was in a car accident that left me paralyzed from the waist down. I will never again play basketball. Looking back on what my dad said that day, I realize now that you never know what's going to happen. You only have today to give that 100 percent to whatever you are doing. I was in the hospital for seven weeks. During that time, I met two young men who would change my life forever.

Both had the same injury but with totally different attitudes. The first was extremely negative. He was never happy and didn't want to do anything for himself. His primary nurse told me that he would probably end up in a nursing home and might eventually die before his time because he wouldn't learn how to take care of himself.

The second young man was completely the opposite. He was always smiling. He would often say to me, "The next time we see each other, we're going to be out of this hospital. We're going to be walking. We're going to run up and give each other a hug. We'll say, 'We made it! It may have taken us forever, but we made it.'"

> "One night I realized that I had to decide whether I was going to get bitter or get better."

One night I realized that I had to decide whether I was going to get bitter or get better. I chose to get better. This decision has made all the difference in my life. I realized that I could do anything I wanted. I might have to do it a little differently because I am in a wheelchair, but if my dream is big enough, the facts won't matter! Dreaming big has paid off for me in that I have realized one of my dreams, which was to become a hairdresser.

You can do anything you want, no matter how big the obstacles. The accident wasn't a bad thing. It was just a difficult thing that has made my life better. As you go through life's experiences and have your ups and downs, always consciously decide to get better.

Three P's to Self-Talk

There are three guidelines you can follow to transform your self-talk. They are:

- Make it **personal.**
- Focus on the **present**.
- Make it **positive**.

Make it a habit to affirm your success, worth, and talent. Positive self-talk is not boastful, arrogant, or egotistical. It's healthy. Let's try this on: Think of yourself within this profession. Your goal is to one day become a talented, successful hair colorist, but you're not quite there. Your self-talk now would be, "I am a talented and skilled hair colorist" or "My clients always love and enjoy the color services I provide." These statements are personal, in the present tense, and positive.

> *Make it a habit to affirm your success, worth, and talent. Positive self-talk is not boastful, arrogant, or egotistical. It's healthy."*

 Another way of transforming your self-talk is to ask questions that will help you find opportunities and discover solutions to situations. These are *forward-focused questions*. The phrasing of your questions affects whether you are focused on the solution or the problem. Forward-focused questions help you to focus forward on the road ahead. They are positively phrased, open-ended questions.

Instead of statements:	**Ask:**
I don't like that.	What do I like or appreciate?
This doesn't work.	What steps can I take to make it work?
This is a terrible situation.	What opportunities do I have in this situation?

Connecting Tip   #3

Choose Success

STEP 1   Cancel the negative. Choose the positive.

STEP 2   Choose your focus.

STEP 3   Manage your self-talk.

STEP 4   Ask forward-focused questions.

Source: Vannoy, Steven W. Ten Greatest Gifts I Give My Children: Parenting from the Heart. Simon and Schuster, 1994.

STEP 4 Choose Love

There are many people in the world who don't like what they do for a living. They complain, criticize, or are bitter. They hate their jobs, dislike their co-workers, and see their customers as interruptions to their days.

Many times people say: "I love everything about my job except certain clients," or "I love everything but my boss," or "I would love my job more if I made more money and had a paid vacation." The secret to success isn't getting everything you want and then loving it. The key is to start by being in love with what you do, to appreciate your teammates, and to willingly serve and help all of your clients. Do all this and you will start getting everything you want. You'll become a magnet and simply pull what you want and love into your life! To be successful in anything you do, you need what the industry legend Sydell Miller describes as *creative love*. Sydell says, "You must love what you do, love whom you do it with, and love whom you do it for."

> *Love is not a noun; it is a verb that requires action."*

Love Is a Verb

 Love is not a noun; it is a verb that requires action. This simply means that you must do the actions of love, even if you don't have the feeling of love. Maybe you don't feel love toward a team member or for your leader, but still do loving things for her, such as shampooing her client or getting her lunch. Respond in loving ways and practice loving actions until they begin to stick. To have the qualities of love in your professional life, you must:

- **Love what you do** — One of the most important steps you can take toward success and happiness is to love what you do. If you aren't doing what you love now, then learn to love it while you search for something you feel passionate about.

  If you observe really successful people, you will notice that they really love what they do. These people attract others like themselves and are inspiring and energizing to be around.

- **Love whom you do it with** — A successful salon is made up of people who are in supportive and healthy relationships with each other. Clients don't want to spend their time or money in a salon where the staff doesn't get along. Cultivate a good relationship with each person on your team. Say, I love my team! I love my clients!

*Say, I love my team!
I love my clients!"*

- **Love whom you do it for** — Who do you think pays your paycheck? If you answered your boss or the salon, think again. Your clients are the ones who ultimately pay. Without clients you will not survive in the salon. Without clients you will not be able to buy food, pay your rent, go on vacation, or buy a car. They are why you exist professionally.

Some Salon Professionals forget this from time to time. They see themselves as more important than their clients. When you put yourself before your clients, your business will stop growing. Clients want to feel loved, nurtured, and supported, and they will search for someone else to love and nurture them when you forget to.

When you learn to love serving your clients, they will repay you with their trust, loyalty, referrals, and money. **Chapter 5** will give you more ideas on how to show your clients that you love them.

Connecting Tip   #4

Choose Love

- Create love in your life.
- Love what you do.
- Love whom you do it with.
- Love whom you do it for.

STEP 5 Be Nice

Another really important recommendation is to simply be nice. We believe that there is a process to becoming nice. Being nice is not just a cliché that is preached in church. Being nice is an attitude that you can choose. It is a personality characteristic that you can learn.

Being nice is a marketing strategy — Customers will spend a lot of money with a hairdresser, a nail technician, a skin care therapist, or in a salon, that is nice. The salon or school that embraces a "be nice" culture will have a major competitive edge. Be Nice is a marketing campaign, business strategy, staff training theme, and customer promise. A "be nice" approach to business builds customer loyalty and your income.

Being nice is an attitude that you can choose."

Being nice is good business — Being nice is not a physical trait that is passed on from your parents. It is something you study. If you are a person who attracts people who love to share their problems and complaints, ask yourself, "Why am I so available for that type of information?"

To begin being nice, you have to eliminate things in your life that blur your perception of what being nice is all about. You have to divorce yourself from people, beliefs, and experiences that cause you to be mean or insensitive. If you love negative drama, you will attract dramatic, negative people who can't wait to tell you how bad their lives are.

Connecting Tip   #5

How to Be Nice
- Fake it.
- Make a list of nice people.
- Find nice mentors.
- Perform random acts of kindness.
- Practice being nice.
- Collect nice stories.

NEEKO

Neeko Abriol is co-owner of Sessions Studio in Pasadena, California. His magazine credits include Elle, Vanity Fair, YM, Us, Esquire, Sports Illustrated, Ebony, Allure, *and others. His hairdressing credits span music videos, feature films, commercials, print advertising, and television. He received the North American Hairdresser of the Year awards in 1997, 1998, and 2000.*

Neeko has made a 360-degree turn in his life. He went from being a gang member dodging bullets, dealing drugs in the inner city of Los Angeles, and escaping the threat of prison, to changing his focus and discovering his passion in the beauty industry.

I grew up in a normal middle-class family in Los Angeles. I had all of the opportunities that everyone else had to go to school and college. I didn't get along with my parents and was considered a "disruptive" child. By the age of 12, I was out, occasionally living with my cousins. I became caught up in a group that was drug-oriented. Eventually I was dealing drugs. Finally, I was arrested with a large amount of cocaine, which potentially could have given me a five-year prison sentence.

While I was waiting for my court date, I decided to make changes. I started to attend motivational classes, read motivational books, and joined a church. At church there was a youth counselor who recommended that I become a barber. I wasn't sure if it was right for me. I wanted to do something that would make a difference and would help people. After checking out some schools, I decided that I was interested. I found a school that I liked. The challenge was that I had no money. I decided to go on a scavenger hunt. I went from salon to salon telling my story. Many people helped me. It was inspiring how people who I didn't know would invest in my future. I raised almost $500 in one week, but still needed about $100 more. I went to one last salon and told my story to a stylist there.

I shared all the details of my past lifestyle, including my arrest and how I wanted to change. I later discovered that stylist was the wife of the district attorney who was prosecuting me.

ABRIOL

That next Monday, I started school. I knew from the start that this was what I wanted to do with my life. I became so focused on what I was learning that I forgot about my pending court case scheduled in four days. I let go of my fear and prayed for peace. I had discovered what I most loved to do and a divine intervention was now in control of my life. That day I walked into court and the D.A. withdrew his plea.

> "I had discovered what I most loved to do, and a divine intervention was now in control of my life. That day I walked into court and the D.A. withdrew his plea."

I went on to work in a salon, making many mistakes and learning a lot in the process. As I followed my passion, I built a successful clientele. I began working with a photographer to document my work. Eventually I interviewed with an agency representing hair, makeup, and styling artists for the fashion and entertainment industry. My first big break came within the music industry. Music companies liked my work with new and upcoming artists.

I love what I do, and I want to share it with others. I believe we are a lot like trees. The fruit that comes from a tree isn't just there to make the tree look good, it is for the benefit of others. I believe it's important to share the fruit with others around me.

I also believe it is important to be mindful of where we plant ourselves. Like a tree, we cannot grow in rocky or shallow soil. We need to be supported, nurtured, and constantly fed. I have learned that it is important to carefully choose who I plant myself near. I choose to associate with others who contribute to my success. I love what I do and surround myself with people who feel the same way.

DEVELOP A
"BE NICE" ATTITUDE

The "be nice" process includes simple steps that can create major results. Begin by trying them on. You will be amazed at the results. Here they are:

① **Fake it** — Eric Fisher, a very successful salon owner in Wichita, Kansas, says there are two reasons he will fire an employee. The first is for stealing.

The second is if they show up to work in a bad mood. He fires them on the spot! But he'll rehire them five minutes later if they leave the salon and come back in a good mood. He asks his staff to fake it until they feel better.

By choosing a career in the salon and beauty industry, you have automatically given up the right to come to school or work in a bad mood. You have chosen a career that is people-focused and your mood affects others around you.

Will you always be in fantastic moods every day? Of course not. There may be days when you are not excited about going to work and times when you don't feel like being nice.

So what do you do on those days? You fake it! You sit in your car for an extra five minutes and crank that fun music and talk yourself out of that bad mood. Then you walk in to start your day as if it were showtime and you were on stage.

② **Find nice mentors** — Nice people are all around you! Perhaps you will find nice mentors in your family, your school, or circle of friends. Look for famous nice people or celebrities to inspire you. Sister Bonnie, whose story is profiled in **Chapter 6**, is an example of a nice mentor. She provides haircut services for those who cannot afford to pay. She is always there to help and assist others. Watch what nice people do and copy it.

③ **Collect nice stories** — Look for stories that combat the negative ones people tend to share. The next time someone starts rambling out her negative drama, start reciting your nice stories. "Did you hear about the wonderful people who all volunteered their time?"

④ **Practice** — Sing songs at full volume in your car. Show gratitude for what you have. Send love notes and thank-you cards. Practice feeling and showing appreciation.

⑤ **Perform random acts of kindness** — Do nice things for friends, loved ones, teammates, and even total strangers just because it's the right thing to do.

⑥ **Develop the language of a nice person** — Nice people are polite. They use kind and considerate words.

Acknowledge people when you see them, thank them, and compliment them. Most of all, go out of your way to be nice.

In an industry where you have to be technically competent and knowledgeable, it is important to also be nice. You can be artistically brilliant, but you'd better be nice.

You can be a gifted sales-person, but you'd better be nice. Choosing to be nice has many benefits, including the satisfaction that you are making a difference in other people's lives.

DAVID WAGNER

Many of the industry's most successful people have started exactly where you are today. They all have their share of humbling experiences. There is no one better to share his story than David Wagner, who is currently the president of a multimillion dollar chain of upscale salons and spas named Juut Salon Spa. His salons are considered among the best in the United States.

David is well known in the industry as a nice guy who will help anyone in need. He rose to the top because he always did his best no matter what goal he was pursuing. He has made it a priority to help others and calls himself a "daymaker."

"Do your best! Do it really, really well!"

When I was ready to graduate from high school, my father asked me what I was going to do with the rest of my life. "I am going to be a hair stylist," I told him with conviction. He simply said, "No, you're not. They don't make any money," which was true in a small town in the 1970s.

I persisted with my vision and attended a prestigious cosmetology school in Minneapolis. I was 18 years old, fresh off the farm and ready to open my own salon, or so I thought. Horst Rechelbacher, the owner, worked in the salon next door and charged $100 for a haircut. Thirty years ago, the average price for a haircut and style in a salon was about $12. "Not bad!" I thought.

Upon graduation from cosmetology school, I was offered my first job with Horst Salons to valet park the customers' cars. You know what? I did it really, really well. In fact, I made more money than some of the hair stylists who worked inside. Then I got a job within the salon, which was great, because it was November in Minnesota!

My new job consisted of shampooing clients and folding towels. Again, I did it really, really well. I did it well enough that Horst asked me to be his personal assistant, working alongside him and catering to his clients. When I finally had completed my training program and became a hairdresser, I decided I wanted to be the best I could be. So I went to Europe to learn from other hairdressing masters. Later, I went on to open my own salons and spas.

Do your best! Do it really, really well! My goal was to do my best and to really service people. This is when I decided to start my professional career as a *daymaker*. Today my goal is to make the day of each person I touch, by doing my very best.

Learn how you can be a daymaker by reading *Life as a Daymaker: How to Change the World Simply by Making Someone's Day.*

MY OUTLOOK
GAME PLAN

BEAUTY

In this chapter you learned about programming yourself into becoming a positive, successful professional. Let's create the first step of your game plan. Make a commitment to program yourself to think positively. **Write your commitment here.**

_____

REFLECT

Think about what fears or obstacles may interfere with keeping your commitment. **Write them here.**

_____

TAKE ACTION

TIME
Review what you spend your time on. Take an inventory of your program.

SNAP OUT OF IT
Cancel negative programming. Create a new program of things that make you happy.

FOCUS
Choose your focus. Manage your self-talk.

LOVE
Love is a verb that requires action. Love what you do. Love whom you do it with. Love whom you do it for.

NICE
Be nice. On down days, fake it.

REACH
Make it your goal to do your best, no matter what the task.

DAYMAKER
Really service people by becoming a "daymaker."

"Live as if you were
to die tomorrow.
Learn as if
you were to
live forever."

Mahatma Gandhi,
Indian leader and philosopher

THINK

Chapter 2

My Brain

We are now in the Information Age. Because of technology, the way you live and do business will constantly transform. Think about the developments in just the past 10 years. Cell phones, e-mail, Web sites, palm pilots, and DVDs are all now a part of our lives. They have revolutionized how we think, get information, and communicate with one another.

Improvement of and changes to current technologies will continue at lightning speed. Just as you think you are mastering one technology, another will be developed. You will adjust, learn, and apply them to your daily life.

In the job market you will be bombarded with new ideas and techniques. At first it may seem a little overwhelming, unless you have a strategy to remember and apply what you are learning.

The good news is that learning is a skill that you can develop and improve. You can learn how to learn faster and make the process more fun. In this chapter you will be introduced to ways of improving your learning and performance skills with easy, fun suggestions to help you become a superlearner.

Take what works for you and try it on. You can't fail. Then leave the rest behind for now. Your success is guaranteed!

Improve the way you learn and perform

Think about:

- What is learning?

- What is my learning style?

- How will I improve my learning skills?

- What is my learning strategy?

Learn about:

- How people learn.

- Your learning style.

- Become a better Learner.

Learn from:

- Dennis James

What Is Learning?

There are many ways to learn. Some people like to learn in very traditional ways, similar to how they learned in high school. Some see learning as a discovery process, and others like to learn by connecting with people. There is no right or wrong way to learn. The key to your success is in figuring out how you like to learn and then getting really good at the process.

> *The key to your success is in figuring out how you like to learn and then getting really good at the process."*

You can quickly learn any new skill to improve your performance by becoming a *superlearner.* Superlearners are people who have mastered the skill of learning. Yes, learning is a skill just like reading or styling hair. Once you learn how to learn, you can confidently tackle any subject with success.

Becoming a superlearner means that you are open and willing to try on new ideas and to let go of what you already think you know. We call this "emptying your cup." Visualize a cup filled to the rim with water. The water represents your current knowledge. Before you can allow more water (knowledge) into your cup, you have to empty some of the old water (ideas) out.

Superlearners are successful because they are open and willing to empty their cups.

There are many beliefs about education that may block your learning. They include believing that:
- You can only learn from an expert or the teacher.
- It's not good to make mistakes.
- You look dumb when you ask questions.
- It is hard to learn new information and skills.
- Cramming your mind full of details is learning.
- Learning is boring and time-consuming.

> *Learning is a life skill that will bring you opportunities for success, satisfaction, and adventure."*

What do *you* believe about learning? Your assumptions may be holding you back from truly enjoying the learning process. Learning is a life skill that will bring you opportunities for success, satisfaction, and adventure. Let's try something on. Let go of how learning is supposed to be and redefine how you will learn.

A New Definition for Learning

 Did you know that you are always learning? As a matter of fact, you cannot *not* learn. You are a learning machine. You just have to know what makes you as the learning machine work at your most efficient capacity.

The way we think and learn is being researched now more than ever before. As new methods of teaching and learning are developed, you will be asked to change as a Learner. Here are some ways you will want to grow:

Learn how to ask questions — Young children are always asking questions. Questioning is an important part of learning. Throughout the process of learning, you should constantly ask questions and persistently search for answers.

Search for the information — Don't wait to be taught, take charge of your learning. Learning is a verb, which means you need to take action. Don't check out during the learning process. Stay focused and learn from your co-workers, classmates, clients, videos, magazines, demonstrations, and lectures.

Define your learning style — There is not just one way to learn. We each have a unique learning style and preferences. Define what works for you as a Learner and do it. Master your unique learning approach, then be flexible and try on new ways to learn.

Acknowledge your feelings while you learn — Learning is emotional as well as intellectual. Your emotions about who you are learning with, how you are learning, and what you are learning can either help you or keep you from learning. Your emotions help you to remember what you have learned. The stronger your feelings about what you are learning, the longer and more vividly you will remember it. Positive learning experiences make you feel happy, interested, and secure. You are motivated and focused. If something is not working and you find yourself not enjoying the process, then change it.

Your emotions help you to remember what you have learned."

The stronger your feelings about what you are learning, the longer and more vividly you will remember it."

Guiding Principles

Educators have taken much of the new research on learning and applied it to school curriculums. They created a list of learning values and beliefs called the *Guiding Principles.* This list may help you to change your beliefs about the learning process and your role as a Learner.

- Education is an adventure of discovery.

- Effective learning starts with a game plan, which helps you to focus on taking action.

- Learning is blocked when fear is present. Let go of your fears and try on what you are learning.

- Making a mistake is not fatal. You make discoveries, not mistakes. Learn to embrace your discoveries and make them part of the learning process.

- You learn best when you are having fun.

- Learning success is based on changing your behavior and beliefs. Learning is a verb, so put your knowledge into action.

- You are uniquely intelligent and have your own style of learning. Find a learning strategy that best fits what you like and how you prefer to learn and follow it. When you honor your special qualities, you automatically become more successful.

- You learn best when you are physically, emotionally, mentally, and creatively involved.

- The learning process is neither good nor bad; it simply is working or not working. If it is working, improve it. If it is not working, change it.

- Recognizing your personal successes encourages you to learn more. Praise and rewards are everyone's best motivators.

- The most effective Learners have learned to think for themselves. They don't wait to be told. They have taken responsibility for what and how they are learning.

Connecting to your future is a journey filled with discoveries, not failures. Adopt thoughts that will keep your learning positive and productive.

> *Learning is a verb, so put your knowledge into action."*

Your Learning Style

Superlearners are successful because they are open and willing to learn. In this section you will learn how to improve as a Learner. Remember that you are learning all the time. Learning is a natural process that is the result of your experiences. Your learning has a cycle that has been outlined by educational expert Bernice McCarthy. Her learning theory explains that we all experience learning in phases that can be defined by four basic questions: *Why? What? How? What if?*

You can improve your learning by asking yourself questions such as:

- **Why** do I need to know this information? **Why** is it important?
- **What** is the information I need to know and master?
- **How** do I learn it? **How** do I perform the steps?
- **What if** I did it differently? **What if** I created my own methods?

Let questions guide your learning. When you are truly interested in something you naturally ask a lot of questions. Your questions guide and help you to learn more. Here is an example of how you can use questions to guide your learning of finger waving.

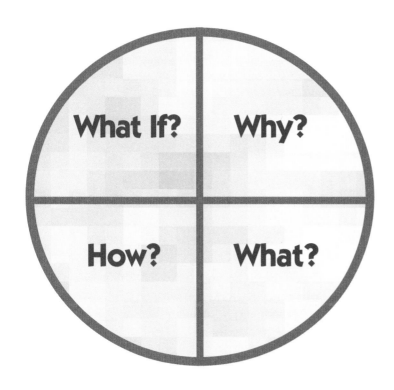

Source: McCarthy, Bernice. 4Mat System. EXCEL, Inc., 1980.

EXAMPLE: FINGER WAVING

Question: **Why do I need to know this information?**

Answer: Finger waving will help you to see and master movement and direction of the hair. It helps you to gain the dexterity you need to perform a variety of hair styling techniques. Answering "why" identifies the benefits you gain from learning.

Question: **What do I need to learn?**

Answer: You need to know about the tools and products to perform a finger wave, where to begin on the head, how to perform the "c" shaping, and how to form alternating ridges and troughs to the wave. Answering "what" identifies the detailed information you need to learn to perform a finger wave.

Question: **How do I perform the steps?**

Answer: During this phase of learning, your focus is on putting your knowledge into action. Your goal is to master the steps to correctly perform a task. Answering "how" identifies step-by-step procedures.

Question: **What if I change it?**

Answer: When you ask "what if" you have gained enough knowledge and skill to creatively change what you have learned. To create the same effect as a finger wave, what if you used a curling iron instead of the styling lotion and comb? (This is called *Marcel Waves*.) Or you could finger wave the crown of the head and then curl the bottom with pin curls.

Improve your comprehension. Answer all four questions each time you learn something new. When you take advantage of each learning phase, you will find that you can learn faster, while having fun.

Connecting Tip   #6

Know Your Learning Style

Knowing your learning style helps you to better manage your learning. The key to success is defining who you are as a Learner. You can change your style by using your new awareness to grow, instead of labeling yourself and resisting change. If it works for you, then do it. If it isn't working, then change it.

There Is No Wrong Way to Learn

You are unique as a Learner because of your personality, approach, and preferences. You may prefer a certain aspect of learning over others. For example, you may prefer to jump right into what you learn, or you may choose to study all of the information thoroughly before you start applying your knowledge. Your unique approach to learning is called your *learning style*.

Your learning style defines how you learn. It describes what you prefer and predicts how you may respond during the learning process. The following are descriptions of four basic learning styles. Read through all the descriptions and check the ones that best describe you. You may select descriptions from different learning styles. It is possible to have more than one learning style.

> **"** *Your unique approach to learning is called your learning style.* **"**

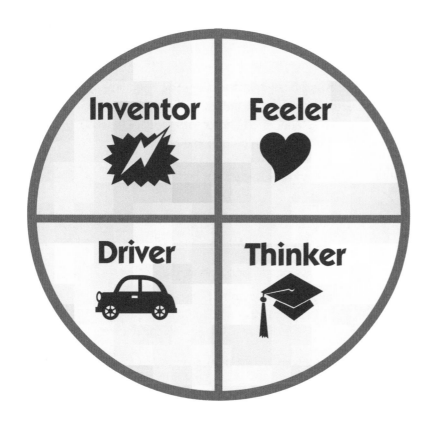

Source: Callahan, Tommy. The Learning System. *JOHN PAUL MITCHELL SYSTEMS, 1995.*

What's Your Learning Style?

Check the traits that describe you —
If you are a Feeler Learner:

Feelers primarily learn by relating to and connecting with others. You perceive the learning process as emotional. When in balance, you love to work in groups and are very social. When out of balance, you withdraw and do not participate.

- [ ] You naturally ask, "Why do I need this information?" or "Why is this important?"
- [ ] You need to know the meaning of what you are learning and how it relates to you.
- [ ] You need to know the benefits of what you are learning.
- [ ] You are social and like to work with partners or in groups while learning.
- [ ] You seek an emotional connection to what you are learning, your teachers, and fellow learners.
- [ ] You learn through relationships.
- [ ] You need to be in a harmonious and cooperative learning environment.
- [ ] You are sensitive to criticism and unsolicited feedback, preferring a gentle approach when being coached.

If you are a Thinker Learner:

Thinkers primarily learn by thinking and assimilating information. You need time to reflect and process what you are learning internally before you apply it. When in balance, you are a detailed and focused listener and Learner. When out of balance, you focus too much on unimportant information, or you become critical.

- [ ] You naturally ask, "What do I need to know to perform better?"
- [ ] You love facts and details.
- [ ] You want an organized learning environment.
- [ ] You want to understand the reason things work.
- [ ] You like things sequential, methodical, logical, and systematic.
- [ ] You need to learn the concepts and facts thoroughly before you are comfortable performing.
- [ ] You may seek perfection.
- [ ] You learn by problem-solving and thinking things through.
- [ ] You like to research and find information.
- [ ] You like to reflect on what you have been learning.
- [ ] You like specific and detailed feedback and coaching.

If you are a Driver Learner:

Drivers learn by doing and actively pursuing new skills. You like taking risks and making discoveries. You see learning as an active process and like to learn things quickly. When you are in balance, you are open to feedback and coaching and like to lead learning activities. When you are out of balance, you can be disruptive and impatient.

- [ ] You naturally ask, "How do I perform it?" or "What are the steps in doing it?"
- [ ] You learn best by doing.
- [ ] You love to jump right in and figure it out. You detest long, drawn-out explanations or lectures.
- [ ] You like to identify step-by-step procedures.
- [ ] You learn best when you are active. You like role-playing, simulations, and rehearsals.
- [ ] You are the first to put things to use when they are useful.
- [ ] You use common sense to problem solve.
- [ ] You want a basic overview of what you are learning and do not need every little detail.
- [ ] You like demonstrations and workshops and welcome hands-on coaching.

If you are an Inventor Learner:

Inventors learn by creating. You love to tweak what you are learning, experiment, and make it your own. You truly think outside of the box. When you are in balance, you add creativity and a fresh perspective. When you are out of balance, you are unfocused, distracted, and all over the map.

- [ ] You naturally ask: "What if I did it differently?" or "What else do I need to learn to be more creative?"
- [ ] You learn best by creating and inventing new methods.
- [ ] You are not satisfied with the traditional ways of using information or performing tasks.
- [ ] You learn by being innovative.
- [ ] You want to explore all of the opportunities.
- [ ] You want to improve what you are learning or create a new way to learn.
- [ ] You like to implement, then improve your work.
- [ ] You learn through experimentation.
- [ ] You like coaching and feedback on the end product and on your creativity.

Did you check more descriptions under one learning style than under the others? If so, that would be your primary learning style. Knowing your learning style will help you identify learning opportunities.

Stretch Your Style

Don't allow your learning to become boring. Step out of your box and stretch your style. Become flexible in your approach to learning and find new ways to learn. For example:

- **If you are a feeler,** take more risks, jump right in, and learn from your discoveries. Be open to more feedback, and try not to take it personally.

- **If you are a thinker**, step out of your box and let go of how things are "supposed to be." Become more creative and explore different aspects of what you are learning.

- **If you are a driver,** try to become more detailed, more like a thinker.

- **If you are an inventor**, learn to work and collaborate with others, become more like a feeler, or become more systematic like a thinker.

By stretching yourself, your learning will become more interesting, and you will become well-rounded. You may discover something about yourself through the process.

Now that you know your style, create a learning strategy that fits your needs. Don't wait for someone to accommodate you. Ask for help, and give your instructor feedback about what you like and how you learn.

By stretching yourself, your learning will become more interesting…"

Connecting Tip   #7

Stretch Your Style

To improve your learning, approach it from various perspectives. If you like to learn as a thinker, try learning as an inventor. We all are a little of all learning types. Bringing out the other styles in your personality will help to deepen your understanding. Become your own learning coach and motivate yourself to become a better Learner.

Learning Strategies

In addition to knowing your learning style, there are other strategies that can help you to become a superlearner. Check what you can do!

Prepare to learn. Preparation is key to enjoying the learning process. It's like stretching prior to working out. You will be far more productive and more likely to retain what you have learned if you are prepared.

Prepare Emotionally

☐ Prepare to learn by letting go of your fears.
☐ Create a learning affirmation statement to focus your thinking.
☐ Find a supportive learning partner.

Prepare Mentally

☐ Preview all learning materials prior to learning. Flip through materials and look for key ideas, skills, and terminology.
☐ Clearly identify your goals.
☐ Stretch your learning style.
☐ Create a visual learning map.

Prepare Physically

☐ Study during your peak times. If you are a morning person, get up early and focus on learning when you are fresh. If you are a night owl, sleep in and study late. Don't force yourself to study when you are tired.
☐ Breathe from your diaphragm—oxygen helps the brain function better.
☐ Feed your body. Eating healthy foods high in vitamins helps you to focus and stay alert. When you are hungry, you are not able to focus.
☐ Create a learning wall and learning space at home. A learning wall is a place you can hang your visual learning maps, affirmations, and goals. Organize your learning space. Make it colorful, clean, and organized. Each morning wake up, stretch, and exercise in front of your learning wall.

Prepare Creatively

☐ Purchase colored markers to create learning maps.
☐ Buy a tape recorder and create audio tapes of key terms that you want to remember.
☐ Create a tape that outlines the key ideas from each chapter of this book, and listen to it frequently.
☐ Take a drawing, beginning art, or art appreciation class. This will help to open up your mind creatively.
☐ Visit salons, museums, hotels, spas, and service-oriented businesses to gather ideas that will help you expand your learning.

DENNIS JAMES

Dennis James began his career in the beauty industry as a hairdresser in 1985 and has built a strong foundation as a designer in top salons in both Beverly Hills and Salt Lake City. He has performed as a platform artist and national educator. Dennis is currently the education director for PAUL MITCHELL THE SCHOOL, PAUL MITCHELL THE SCHOOL PARTNER SCHOOL PROGRAM, and is a JPMS master associate.

"Learn how to learn, and you will love what you learn." How ironic that I would be the one sharing information on how to learn and get the most out of your education. You see, I wasn't the ideal student throughout elementary school, high school, and cosmetology school. Fortunately, I had people in my life who pushed me to take advantage of the many learning opportunities all around me.

Something happened to me in the first grade that would affect me for many years to come. My first grade teacher told me that I couldn't read. Because she was the authority, I accepted what she said as fact; however, I was confused. I knew that I could read certain subjects, especially the ones that were interesting to me. I also liked to learn, especially when the information was delivered in fun and interesting ways. It was very important to me, even at an early age, to see the relevance of what I was learning.

I did not conform to what was considered a "good student." My self-esteem and confidence suffered. I have since discovered that I was more successful as a Learner when I learned in ways that were compatible with my preferences. After this discovery, I became passionate about my learning process.

> **"I did not conform to what was considered a 'good student.' My self-esteem and confidence suffered."**

Fortunately, I was able to connect with many mentors who saw value in the learning process. These amazing coaches helped me to commit myself to a lifelong learning journey. I was taught to never discount someone's ability to learn, especially my own. I started to share my story with others and discovered my situation was not unique. Many Learners who I mentored had similar early learning experiences.

Today I coach trainers on how to be Learning Leaders. I first teach how to learn. I believe that once you become a better Learner, you in turn become a better communicator, parent, friend, and leader. I have seen many personal transformations as people became better Learners.

BE A BETTER LEARNER

Dennis James shares these tips to becoming a better Learner.

① "Say it"—
I like to share what I have learned with others. I have noticed that my retention is improved when I teach someone else what I have learned. If I miss the chance to share what I have learned within one week, I don't remember it as vividly.

② "Remember it"—
I have learned that if I return to my notes for several days after my learning process, my recall is much greater than had I just read and discarded them. Find a strategy that helps you to remember.

Whether it is note-taking, creating your own audio tapes, making a wall of Post-it® notes, or just doing something over and over, spark your memory.

③ "Love it"—
Let go of all of the criticism you have about yourself. Find ways to love your learning process. It is more fun to let go and explore than it is to criticize or judge.

The bottom line is, "Learn how to learn, and you will love what you learn."

> *Find ways to love your learning process."*

Connecting Tip   #8

Create a Superlearner Strategy

- Preview materials prior to learning.
- Receive new information in a variety of ways.
- Practice what you have learned using a variety of rehearsal methods.
- Implement and improve upon what you have learned.

Sensory Learning Strategies

Think of the ways you prefer to learn. Do you like to listen and discuss concepts, watch videos or demonstrations, or jump in and learn from your discoveries? Select from the following activities:

Learning by WATCHING and SEEING

- [ ] Work with partners and have them act out steps as you read. (Then switch).
- [ ] Watch demonstrations, a video, or DVDs.
- [ ] Draw pictures or diagram steps.
- [ ] Visualize or mentally rehearse the steps.
- [ ] Create flash cards with key terminology or create procedure cards for each service type.

Learning from LISTENING, SPEAKING, and DISCUSSING

- [ ] Listen to instructional audio tapes as you take a walk.
- [ ] Listen to soft music as you study.
- [ ] Create a tape of what you read, and then listen to it before a test or evaluation.
- [ ] When performing a service or technique, talk through each step as you perform it.
- [ ] Work with partners and have them talk you through the steps or discuss the information.
- [ ] Teach someone else what you learn. Pretend as if you are the teacher and teach them what you know.

Learning from PERFORMING, EXPERIMENTING, and TOUCHING

- [ ] Perform a technique step by step, while following an instructional video.
- [ ] Use a variety of props and different materials. Shave a mannequin head and place straws on the head to learn about elevation. Use colored markers and watercolor paints to learn about color theory.
- [ ] Squeeze a soft squishy toy during a lecture and sip some tea or coffee. Take time to engage all of your senses when learning.

Learning from SMELLING sweet success

- [ ] Enhance your long-term memory with scents.
- [ ] As you learn, find your favorite aroma and smell it often. Wear your favorite aroma on the big test day. You will be amazed!
- [ ] Citrus fragrances stimulate and help you to concentrate. Floral and sweet aromas usually have a calming effect. Use scents to stimulate you.

Practice and Apply What You Learned

During the practice phase you have an opportunity to really grow and master your learning. You may find that the more focused you are when you practice, the faster and better you will learn a new skill.

Learning is not beneficial unless you put what you have learned to use. As you complete the learning process, ask yourself, "What did I learn from this?" and "How can I put this information to good use?"

Finally, we recommend that you make learning part of your daily life. Let go of distractions that keep you from improving your performance. Spend time each week building your knowledge, your skills, and, most importantly, your attitude. When you learn in ways that are compatible with your learning style, you will:

- Learn faster.
- Have more fun.
- Recall what you learned.
- Improve your performance.

Connecting Tip   #9

Be a Lifelong Learner

- Read motivational, informational, and professional development books, magazines, and materials.

- Listen to audio learning programs.

- Attend ongoing learning seminars and classes.

MY BRAIN
GAME PLAN

THINK
In this chapter you learned about learning and learning styles. Let's create the second step of your game plan. Make a commitment to discover and improve your learning style. **Write your commitment here.**

_____

REFLECT
Think about what fears or obstacles may interfere with keeping your commitment. **Write them here.**

_____

TAKE ACTION

REINVENT
Make room for learning new ideas and information.

ASK
Learn how to ask questions, especially why, what, how, and what if?

STRETCH
Recognize and use your learning style, then stretch yourself to try other ways of learning.

LEARN
Learning is an active process. Take control and become an active participant. Prepare yourself to learn.

FOLLOW
Follow the Guiding Principles to make your learning more worthwhile.

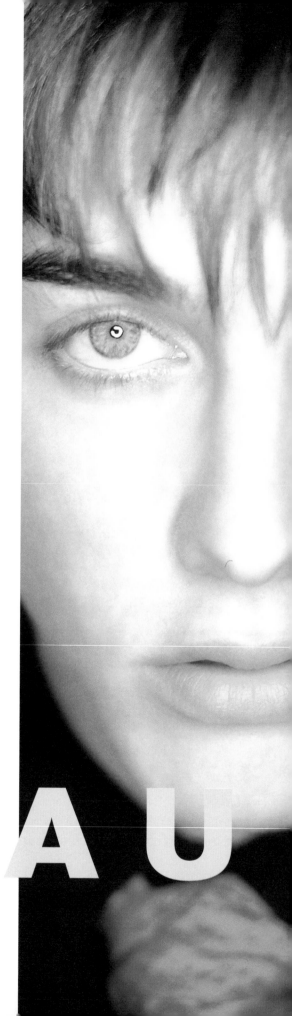

"Beauty has many forms of expression. Discover your beauty, own it, improve it, and appreciate it. It is who you are — a unique expression of life."

PAUL MITCHELL THE SCHOOL

BEAU

Chapter 3

My Style

If you want to "play big," you have to look and act like a successful professional. Your personal style and ability to build relationships are key to how much money you make and how successful you are within your profession.

In this chapter we will explore how to create the image of a knowledgeable and successful beauty consultant—your new role. You will focus on developing the way you express yourself through your style and behavior.

Beauty is the result of the personal attitudes you have about yourself and others. Beauty comes in all sizes, colors, and styles. A common quality of people who recognize their beauty is confidence.

Confident people focus on their assets and work to improve areas of personal dissatisfaction. You'll take an inventory to define your current personal style, then develop a plan to refine it so that you attract success.

Discover your unique style and image

Think about:

- What is my personal style?

- What can I do to refine my image?

- What can I do to take better care of myself?

- What must I do to be successful?

Learn about:

- You're beautiful!

- Your image programming.

- Your style.

- Your professional life skills.

Learn from:

- Stephanie Kocielski

- Melissa Jaqua

- Jay Eklund

You're Beautiful!

With your decision to enter the beauty profession, you must also make a commitment to being "beautiful." Beauty is a quality that starts from within and is a reflection of your feelings and thoughts. Beauty is a frame of mind. It is your attitude, as well as how you look. Being a new beauty professional means that your days of self-loathing and body-hating must end. Now!

Let's begin by reviewing your past, identifying inner messages that may hold you back, and changing your body talk.

> **"** *Beauty is a quality that starts from within and is a reflection of your feelings and thoughts."*

Beauty Is Inherited

We all inherit our body types and features from our family. We can also inherit our attitudes about our bodies from the messages we hear as we grow up. Think back to your childhood and teenage years. What did you hear about your body? What did others say about you? What did you think about yourself?

You grew up listening to your family talking about their bodies and yours. The messages you heard can affect how you currently feel about yourself. However, you have a choice to accept some thoughts and release others.

BODY TALK

Which of the following was part of your family's body talk?

Did you hear...
- I'm so fat
- I wish I had longer legs
- She's so plain—luckily she has a great personality
- You're kind of skinny

Or did you hear...
- I'm beautiful
- You are perfect just the way you are
- In our family, we think voluptuous is beautiful
- Your body is beautiful and healthy

Were your family members...
- Constantly on a diet or eating unhealthy foods
- Uncomfortable with body image
- Critical of others and especially you

Or did they...
- Eat healthy and live balanced lifestyles
- Love themselves and appreciate their bodies
- Compliment and encourage you

Identify Your Inner Messages

You can decide whether or not to allow negative messages from your past to affect you in the present. How do you currently feel about your body and image? Do you feel confident, happy, and beautiful, or are you critical and dissatisfied with how you look?

In **Chapter 1** we talked about programming yourself. The first step to defining and refining your image is to reprogram your thoughts and redirect your self-talk about your body. Complete the following statements:

- **I think my body is:**
  For example: too short, out-of-shape, or beautiful and healthy.

- **Things I say to others about my body or image include:**
  I'm fat. My nose is too big. I feel ugly today. Or I feel and look great.

Do your statements reflect an attitude of self-assurance or an attitude that lacks confidence? Your attitudes about yourself and your image are extremely important to how you relate to your co-workers, leaders, and clients. Successful people in the beauty industry are self-assured and comfortable with themselves. As you enter the industry, realize that you have a new role. Your role is to be a beauty expert. You must be knowledgeable and skilled at helping yourself and others look and feel more beautiful.

Remember that before you can make physical improvements, you must first change your programming. If your thoughts about yourself are not complimentary, take steps to redirect your self-talk to be positive.

> *Do your statements reflect an attitude of self-assurance or an attitude that lacks confidence?"*

CREATE A MORE
POSITIVE YOU

❶ Let go — Stop blaming your past and your genetics or making excuses that keep you from feeling physically good about yourself.

❷ Make "I am" statements — Write down and frequently review your positive "I am" statements, like "I am beautiful."

❸ Take action — Examine undermining lifestyle habits and create a plan to change them. Stop smoking, exercise, and eat right.

❹ Focus on goals — Create image goals. Focus on personal image goals rather than self-criticism.

❺ Take care — Some people take better care of their cars than they do of their bodies. Get or give yourself regular facials, manicures, and pedicures. Treat your body with respect.

❻ Wake up — Create a healthy morning routine. Include stretching, light exercise, visualizations of how you want to look, and a daily review of your image goals.

❼ De-stress — Choose to release stress in ways that do not undermine your image. Replace stress habits, like smoking or snacking, with healthy habits, such as deep breathing or stretching.

❽ Clean — Clean and unclutter your personal spaces.

❾ Make time for yourself — Learn to enjoy being alone. Read and listen to your favorite music. Spend time with supportive and healthy friends and family.

❿ Focus and forgive — Practice every day and forgive yourself if you get sidetracked.

Connecting Tip   #10

Love Your Body

- Identify self-limiting thoughts and self-talk.

- Redirect your words and actions by creating positive "I am" statements.

- Practice positive "body talk."

STEPHANIE KOCIELSKI

Stephanie Kocielski is a master associate with John Paul Mitchell Systems, artistic director of a Robert Cromeans salon, and a full-time working hairdresser. Stephanie's work has appeared on the cover of many leading national and international magazines. She is also in charge of hiring, training, and providing creative direction for the Robert Cromeans Salon teams.

Upon entering the beauty world, you are given the choice of success or failure. A belief in yourself and your abilities will determine that outcome. Confidence will propel you faster through "the game." Your success lies in your image and how you feel about yourself.

As hairdressers, we have the ability to make others look and feel great. Our profession gives us the opportunity to find the beauty in others and bring it to the surface. But it all begins within you. It is important to realize that others will be looking at you, just as you are looking at them.

Society tries to dictate the standards of beauty. Forget what society dictates and create your own standard. Whether you're blonde, brunette, short, tall, small, or large, find a place where you are comfortable and move toward it. Create an image for yourself that you want others to see and respect. For example, I know that I will never be perceived as the "small girl," or known as the "pretty one." Yet, I am comfortable with who I am, and I feel it shows in the image I project.

Early in life I made the conscious choice to be successful and to become the greatest hairdresser that I could be. That is what I want to be: confident, successful, and professional.

> "Our profession gives us the opportunity to find beauty in others and bring it to the surface."

Your hair, dress, and image should reflect the environment in which you work. In the salon culture where I work, we have a dress code that requires we wear black. This sets the tone for our collective image. Our individual personalities and attitudes, however, are reflected in the way we style our hair, do our makeup, and dress. What our clients see when they visit the salon is a strong team of talented, self-assured individuals.

Be as big as you can be, dream of success, work hard, and all great things will come. I would personally like to thank my mentors Robert and Margaret Cromeans for constant guidance, love, and inspiration, and Susanne Chadwick for giving a New Jersey girl a shot.

You Are a Walking Billboard

Change your mind and talk and you can achieve a balanced, more beautiful image. Remember that your number one, most important "marketing tool" is you. You are like a walking billboard that says, "This is who I am and how I think." Beauty is an attitude, a quality, and decision you make each day. So make sure that you are a successful, balanced, and beautiful person who knows what you want to become.

When you refine your image, you will attract and retain clients who like and are comfortable with who you are, even if they look considerably different from you. Think for a moment: Would you trust a dentist without teeth? No? Then how can you play the role of a successful, knowledgeable image expert if you have not yet mastered your own image?

> *Beauty is an attitude, a quality, and decision you make each day."*

Your Style

Now create your style. We will help you identify your current style and help you to fine-tune it for your new role.

To define *style* more clearly, we asked Louis Atkins from the Gene Juarez Salon in Seattle, Washington, to share what they look for when they hire new staff. He said, "There are three major elements we look for when we hire people. We look at their attitude, their skills, and their image."

Attitude — The most obvious criterion is a positive attitude. Two things indicate a positive and passionate attitude: being excited about what you are doing and intensely focused on your work. Everyone expresses passion and attitude differently. Some are cheerleaders, while others are quiet and focused. Both styles of expression work.

Skills — Technical skills and communication skills are essential. Gene Juarez Salons retrain everyone who enters the organization. They hire a person who has a method to how she approaches her work. They believe that if she has a systematized approach to her work, her methods can be improved through in-salon training programs.

Image — Future Professionals must have a defined image. They must put thought into how they look. There are three basic images that work within the salon and spa environment. They are categorized as dramatic, classic, and fashion forward.

- *Dramatic* is unique, expressive, or edgy. It is not offensive, grunge, ripped, or outdated. This style is found in fine vintage clothing shops or specialty shops.

- *Classic* is simple, clean-lined, basic, conservative, and timeless. It is not uncomfortable, outdated, mismatched, unironed, or faded. Look for it in quality department stores or shops.

- *Fashion forward* is trendy, current, or hip. It does not overly expose the body and is not impractical. This style is featured in top fashion magazines and on fashion runways.

A great professional image must be comfortable and pleasing to most people. When an image type is out of balance or unkempt, it offends clients or makes them uncomfortable. Your goal is to attract clients, not drive them away.

Connecting Tip   #11

Reprogram Your Self-Image

- Choose healthy foods and balanced lifestyle habits.

- Educate yourself and learn how to create a beautiful image.

- Take care of your entire body.

- Practice every day. Forgive yourself if you get sidetracked.

TALK TO YOUR
CLOTHES

Think about your image goals and make conscious choices about the things you will wear to work or school. Before you put something on for the day ask yourself, "Does this make me feel and look good?" If it doesn't make you look or feel good, then why would you want to keep it, let alone wear it?

Now it's confession time. Do you have mistakes in your closet? Do you have things that should be recycled? If the answer is yes, then here's what you do:

Divide and Conquer

Go piece by piece and separate your clothing into two piles:

PILE ❶
"I look and feel good" pile, a.k.a. the "looking fabulous" pile.

PILE ❷
"what was I thinking?" pile, a.k.a. the "I haven't worn it in years" pile.

Take Inventory

Take inventory of the "fabulous" pile and again categorize the clothing into two new piles:

PILE ❶
Clothing that is acceptable to wear to school or work.

PILE ❷
Clothing that is acceptable to wear only during your personal time.

Inventory Management

Now work at developing and organizing the new pile of the clothing you plan to wear to school or work. Go through all of your clothing, shoes, and accessories and look for stains, tears, and damage. Before you place it back into your closet, repair it, clean and iron it, or polish and shine it. If you cannot repair it, clean it or shine it, then throw it away or recycle it.

Make Room for Your New Image

Put everything from your "what was I thinking?" pile in a bag and give it to someone who really needs it. This will give you room for new clothes.

Professional Wardrobe Choices

Your goal is to look and act like a successful, knowledgeable image consultant. As you look at your wardrobe choices, ask yourself, "What am I promoting to current and future clients?" and "How do I want to be perceived?" You promote and sell beauty, style, and image. This means you have to always support what you sell and invest a percentage of your earnings in your image, just as a teacher spends a percentage of income on educational materials or a lawyer spends money on a legal reference library. It is important to budget for your clothing, shoes, and personal items, as you will always be updating your style.

Dress Code

Most schools or salons have established image guidelines, called a *dress code*, to help their teams support their clients' experience. The number one frustration of salon and school owners and managers is getting their staff and students to follow image guidelines. Following the dress code is an easy way to support the business and create great working relationships with your leaders.

Why a dress code? An established standard of dress provides continuity and consistency that helps clients feel more comfortable. Dress codes are not meant to squelch your creativity, but rather make your decision about what to wear easier.

Image and wardrobe are tools of the trade. If you do not like to wear makeup, style your hair each day, or invest money in clothing, then you should choose another career. Your image is a prerequisite for success in this business.

Take time to read and study the dress code. Make it your goal to look your best within the guidelines. The following are examples of the professional image guidelines PAUL MITCHELL THE SCHOOL has in place for its Future Professionals. Use them as a guide if your school or salon does not have any in place.

Benefits of Cleaning Up Your Wardrobe

- You won't be tempted to wear something that undermines your image.

- You'll be able to manage your wardrobe better.

- It will take less time to get ready in the morning.

- You will be able to see the holes in your wardrobe, so that when you shop, you buy items that fit your image.

- You won't mistakenly put something on that is ripped, smelly, or stained.

ORGANIZE YOUR WARDROBE

Save time getting ready for your day by following these wardrobe organizational tips.

❶ In your closet — Sort and hang your clothes into sweaters, shirts, pants, skirts, dresses, and jackets.

❷ Hang everything in two categories — Put things you can wear to school or work separate from things you wear during your personal time. Don't forget to do the same with your shoes.

❸ Organize accessories — Stash belts, scarves, hats, and purses into plastic see-through boxes.

❹ Organize your drawers — Separate socks, underwear, pajamas, and personal items. If you don't have drawers, buy more plastic see-through boxes.

What to Wear

Clothing
- Clothing must be professional, clean, stain-free, and mended or properly altered.
- Wear dark pants, dresses, or skirts.
- Wear a black or white fashionable shirt, blouse, or top.
- Wear company logo T-shirts only.

Shoes
- Cosmetologists should wear dark shoes that are clean, polished, professional, and comfortable.
- Estheticians should wear white, clean, polished, comfortable, and professional soft-soled shoes.

Hair and cosmetics
- Clean and style your hair prior to arriving at school or the salon.
- Apply cosmetics prior to arriving at school or the salon, using trend-appropriate makeup techniques.

What Not to Wear
- Tennis shoes, gym shoes, or foot thongs.
- Jeans or clothes made of jean material.
- Tank tops.
- Sweatpants and sweatshirts.
- Printed T-shirts, other than your company's logo T-shirts.
- Short skirts that fall above the fingertips.
- Shorts, including spandex or biking shorts.

MELISSA JAQUA

Melissa Jaqua's internationally acclaimed photo work and superior talent with multicultural hair have earned her the prestigious North American Hairstyling Award. Extending her knowledge of "art and business" worldwide, Melissa's stage performances have been internationally showcased. She truly is an inspirational artist with a unique approach to everything she does, giving her a style all her own.

Personal image is the natural evolution that comes from combining your moods, your clothing choices, and your self-confidence to express your inner self. I found this to be my most creative outlet. My image choices are based on how I feel and what I want to nonverbally say about myself in that moment.

Through using different fabrics, textures, and accessories, I can create any image and mood I want. When I choose what I want to wear each morning, I ask myself, "What mood am I in today and do I want to enhance it or change it?" I also think about people I will be seeing that day and how I want them to perceive me.

Have you ever woken up feeling uncreative or uninspired but still had a full day scheduled? Maybe you were really tired. That's when you want to ditch the darker colors or more conservative clothes and reach for the brighter colors or more creative pieces in your closet.

Grab some fun accessories and put something really cool together. It will not only change your image, but it will also enhance your mood and creativity.

> **"You have the power to create the image you want, as well as influence the way people perceive and respond to you."**

If I know I'm going to be meeting with people who are responsible for helping my business grow, I might choose an outfit that looks a little stronger with a cleaner cut. I may purposely wear a stronger shade of lipstick to subconsciously command more attention to what I am saying. You have the power to create the image you want, as well as influence the way people perceive and respond to you. The key is to be versatile. Some people have one look all the time, and that's their signature style. It's important to find your image niche and work it.

Being an artist and someone who gets bored very easily, I tend to mix things up a lot. I buy tops and bottoms to make one complete look, and then have fun finding ways to mix them up with other pieces in my closet. I think this is a true creative expression. Your personal choices and wardrobe combinations help you create a unique image.

LOOK FABULOUS WITH
MELISSA JAQUA

① **"Experiment"** — There are many times when I question what I've put together and you may too, but that's when you have to be confident in your choices. Experimenting with fresh aspects of your image may make you feel uncomfortable. It is important to stretch yourself. Sometimes your experiments may work and sometimes they may not.

② **"Accessorize"** — If you are on a budget, invest in accessories. Many times it's just a matter of adding a really cool pair of hose or the right hat or necklace. Apply your makeup or nail polish in a new way or choose colors that you haven't tried before. Remember, it's only temporary, so go for it!

③ **"Combat boredom with new combinations"** — If you're bored with what's in your closet, try new combinations. Find unusual ways to wear articles of clothing or accessories. Wear contrasting patterns together. Alter your clothes by cutting off the sleeves or changing the length. The possibilities are only limited by your personal creativity.

④ **"Find an image mentor"** — Look at fashion magazines or magazines featuring your favorite singers or actors. Celebrities have some of the greatest images because they get help from the best professional wardrobe stylists.

Don't be afraid of looking like a clone. No matter how hard you try to copy them, your look will always come out different and even more unique because it is your personal style of expression.

⑤ **"Have a good hair day"** — Hair is one of the most versatile elements of your image. As part of choosing a career in the field of fashion, it's practically illegal to stay committed to the same hair style for more than a single season. Your hair must also be as healthy as possible. Healthy looking hair always complements your image.

Connecting Tip   #12

Consciously Create Your Style

- Determine your style and image goals.

- Choose appropriate clothing, accessories, and shoes that portray success.

- Follow your salon or school dress code.

JAY EKLUND

Jay Eklund is a successful stylist and artistic director for Gadabout Salons and Spas located in Tucson, Arizona, and is a national educator with Franesi Italian Style team.

All my life I had been destined to shop. I remember being in junior high and having my three female cousins lead me to the dressing room to try on things they would pick off the rack for me. The problem was that I was one of two boys being raised by a single hairdresser mom. The sale rack was my only shot at staying in style.

After beauty school, I worked as an assistant at an upscale salon and spa. We all took an educational trip to Chicago and, like any good group of hairdressers, did some major shopping. I observed what the others were buying. I was prompted by a senior stylist to try on a pair of boots. After a lot of coaxing, I made the purchase.

I realized that money does buy quality. Those boots were very comfortable and versatile, too. That buying experience made me realize that I felt great wearing comfortable, quality shoes when I had to be on my feet all day. I was determined to figure out how to buy quality from that day forward, even though I didn't know how I would afford it. About a year later, I was flipping through a magazine and fell in love with a pair of Gucci loafers.

They were everything I wanted my image to say! I tore the page out and wrote a note saying, "If anyone is thinking about getting me a Christmas present, these would be just fine." I put it in the back room of the salon. Instead of the shoes, my boss gave me something that was more powerful. She gave me a few of Winn Claybaugh's and Gene Stampora's tapes. I was given the opportunity to see one of Winn's seminars and speak with him. My eyes opened to all the possibilities the world had to offer.

> **"I learned that I held the power to go anywhere and get anything I desired."**

I started to understand "If it's to be. . . it's up to me!" One day after listening to my tape on the way to work, I went straight to the back room and took that picture of the shoes off the board. I took that picture home and I taped it to my closet door. Every day as I got dressed, I saw it hanging there. My focus created the determination to work toward my goal of getting those shoes. It didn't take long until I was actually slipping my new shoes on to go to work.

I learned that I held the power to go anywhere and get anything I desired. All I had to do was identify my goal and never lose sight of it.

Acting the Role

Your image is not just the way you look, but also the way you talk and act. In our final segment you will learn about professional behavior and what is required to be successful. Make a promise to yourself and your team to contribute all you can and to act like a successful image professional.

Most schools and salons have a list of guidelines that define and clarify successful behavior. Guidelines assist and direct you in developing professional life skills. Take time to study your school or salon rules.

Make a promise to yourself and your team to contribute all you can and to act like a successful image professional."

Golden Rules

1. Be on time. Always!
2. Always be in a great mood. Fake it when necessary.
3. Come to work prepared.
4. Be informed. Read all memos and information.
5. Gossip is not allowed.
6. Hold each other accountable by the 24-Hour Rule.
7. Resolve all personal challenges with love.
8. Go to the decision-maker with any apparent unsolvable challenges. Use the "Go in Asking" Rule.
9. Be knowledgeable, literate, and articulate.
10. Always "look the part" of an impeccable professional in a classic, dramatic, or fashion forward image.
11. Always be professional.
12. Do not get personally involved with your teachers or clients.
13. Personal lives remain personal.

⏰ 24-HOUR RULE

Respond to all communications from your team within 24 hours. Let go and resolve all challenges with team members within 24 hours.

ACTING LIKE A SUCCESSFUL
PROFESSIONAL

❶ Attendance and documentation — Be there every day. Show up at least 20 minutes before your class or your first appointment. Be consistent about documenting your time.

❷ Professional image — Support your salon or school dress code. Make it a goal to dress beyond your means. Buy less but buy quality—your clients will notice.

❸ Clean environment — Create a beautiful, clean, and appealing environment to work, learn, and service your clients in. To learn more, refer to the 5 Senses Program in **Chapter 5**.

❹ Communication — Learn to clearly and positively communicate with your clients, your team, and your leaders. Improve your verbal and nonverbal communication skills, including listening. Learn more about communication skills by reading **Chapter 5**.

❺ Learning participation — Show up for classes, educational events, and shows ready to learn, explore, and contribute. Your role is to learn, not criticize. Take home at least one new technique and apply it to bettering your business.

❻ Ready, set, or fake it — Arrive at school or work ready to service your clients and in a great mood. Always act as if you are in a great mood, excited to learn, and focused on your clients even on bad days. Learn to fake it. When you fake positive behavior, you eventually feel better and become more positive.

❼ Code of conduct — Many salons and schools have a code of conduct. Following it prevents conflicts, shows respect for your fellow stylists, and helps you maintain your professional behavior.

❽ The 24-Hour Rule — The 24-Hour Rule is a guideline for responding to e-mail, messages, and requests. Be respectful of others' time and respond within 24 hours.

❾ "Go In Asking" Rule — "Go in asking" is a communication technique taught by Gene Juarez. The technique is used to resolve conflict among team members. When we are in conflict with another team member, rather than jumping to conclusions and blaming, we go in asking questions with the intent to make things better. To do this we must first not assume, judge, or attack the other person. Next, we ask the person to discuss the issue privately and one-on-one. The final step is to ask questions such as, "Would you mind sharing with me what happened the other day?" or "Could we talk about . . .?"

❿ Make a pledge — Your style is a blend and balance of how you feel about yourself, how you dress, and your attitude. Make a pledge to fine-tune your style.

MY STYLE
GAME PLAN

BEAUTY

In this chapter you learned about developing a style that is uniquely yours. Let's create the third step of your game plan. Make a commitment to develop your personal style.
Write your commitment here.

_____

REFLECT

Think about what fears or obstacles may interfere with keeping your commitment. **Write them here.**

_____

TAKE ACTION

TALK
Replace your negative self-talk about your image and body with positive body talk.

RELEASE
Let go of blaming your past and your genetics. Get rid of excuses.

REPLACE
Adopt a positive and healthy lifestyle. Replace unhealthy habits with healthy ones. Clean and organize your house; throw out unhealthy foods.

IMAGINE
Determine which style best fits your personality. Create an image collage outlining each style.

ORGANIZE
Take inventory of your wardrobe, shoes, and accessories. Organize your wardrobe. Follow the dress code in your school or salon.

ACT
Look and act like a successful professional. Follow the Golden Rules, use the 24-Hour Rule, and always "go in asking."

"The beauty professional

is an artist,

a craftsman, and a

business professional.

Success requires

precision tools,

innovative products,

and business-building

promotional materials."

PAUL MITCHELL THE SCHOOL

BUILD

Chapter 4

My Gear

Beauty is an art and a craft. As you gain experience, you will discover that there are many forms of expression within the beauty industry ranging from the ultra-artistic work showcased in competitions, shows, and magazines, to the beautiful and practical street wear launched by product manufacturing and salon companies. Beauty is part artistry and part craft. It is a skill you can learn and expand to a high level of artistry.

No matter what your interest or focus, you are fundamentally a "craftsman." And just like any other craft, such as cabinet-making or jewelry designing, you must have the right tools to produce a beautiful product.

Knowing how to get, use, and maintain the tools of the trade is critical to your success. In this chapter you will learn about promotional tools, like portfolios and business cards, and technical tools needed for hairdressing, hair coloring, makeup, skin care, and nail care services. Learn from some of the best veteran industry professionals who will share their picks of the best tools you will want to invest in.

As a professional, you will continually invest in new tools and learn to use them so that you may be at the top of your craft, always learning, growing, and developing new ways to create and serve.

Get and maintain the tools of the trade

Think about:

- Why is it important to invest in quality tools?

- What is a stylebook and how do I create one?

- What is a portfolio and how do I create one?

- How do I create promotional and business tools?

- What tools do I need to perfect my craft?

Learn about:

- Your promotional tools.
- The tools of the trade.

Learn from:

- David Stanko
- Laini Reeves

Promotional Tools

The kit you were issued during your first days of school is your initial investment in your future business. These tools, however, are just the starting point of what you will need to successfully build your business. In addition to your technical tools, you need promotional tools. These include the following:

A résumé — is used as a record of your work and educational experience and a means to promote yourself when looking for employment. An introductory letter must be included with the résumé.

A business card — is the tool you will use every day to promote your business and build your clientele.

A stylebook — is a book of images collected from various magazines and creatively arranged into a photo album-styled portfolio. You use this important visual tool to communicate with your clients.

A portfolio — is a book of images you personally develop and photograph that is used to promote you to the media to secure work in the professional world.

Your Résumé

Your résumé is an outline of who you are, what your goals are, and a history of your past work and educational experience. Think of your résumé as your personal promotional flyer. Keep it short, between one and two pages, and to the point. It should contain:

- Personal information
- Career goals
- Educational background
- Activities and accomplishments
- Work experience
- References

Pamela Miller

1234 Grand Road, Delafield, Wisconsin 53072
Phone: (517) 299-3000   E-mail: pjmiller@mail.com

Career Objective: To obtain a position in a salon where I may build my business and clientele. To grow with my team.

Education: PAUL MITCHELL THE SCHOOL
1534 Adams Avenue
Costa Mesa, California 92626
Cosmetology Course, Graduated June 11, 2000

John Marshall High School
6843 West Grantosa Drive
Milwaukee, Wisconsin 53218
High School Diploma, Graduated 1998

Activities: PAUL MITCHELL THE SCHOOL
Student Council leader
Design Team member
Participated in Signature Gathering student presentation
Attended trade shows

Accomplishments: Hair designs published in school marketing literature
Top product sales awards
Maintained and serviced successful clientele while in school
Submitted work to NAHA Student Photo Competition

Work History: Salon New
2223 Adams Avenue
Costa Mesa, California 92626
Service Coordinator, June 1999-June 2000

Louisa's Restaurant
1333 West Newport Beach Road
Newport Beach, California 92630
Server, July 1998-May 1999

Fresh Clothing Boutique
2222 Brookfield Road
Brookfield, Wisconsin 53076
Sales Consultant, June 1996-January 1998

References:
(Optional)   James Smith, owner of Salon New
Phone: (929) 246-0000

Kathy Jansen, instructor, PAUL MITCHELL THE SCHOOL
Phone: (801) 374-5111

Dennis James, professional mentor
Phone: (222) 576-2500

Your Résumé

Before you begin writing your résumé, gather all of the information you need to create a complete overview of what you have accomplished. Be sure to include the correct spelling of all names and locations as well as accurate dates, phone, fax, e-mail, cell phone, and address information.

Heading — List your full name, address, phone numbers, fax, and e-mail addresses where you may be reached. Always include your area code.

Career objective — Think about the type of position you are interviewing for and your goals and interests. Create a one or two sentence objective that reflects your goals.

Education — List the names of the schools you have attended, the dates of attendance, and course of study. List your most recent education first, then work back to high school.

Activities — Emphasize activities or accomplishments that relate to the position you are applying for. Keep your list short. If you have a longer list of accomplishments or you would like to list all of the seminars you have attended, create a reference list that you refer to in your résumé.

Accomplishments — Briefly describe significant accomplishments while in school or in previous positions.

Work experience — Create a chronological list of employers starting with your most recent job. State the name of the company, the position you held, and the dates when you were employed.

References — List the people who the potential employer may contact to provide information about you. Be sure to call the people you plan to list to ask their permission and check their availability. You may want to use mentors, past employers, or instructors.

Career Objective Examples

- To develop my skills and knowledge working as a stylist.

- To build my clientele as a stylist in a creative and innovative salon environment.

- To develop and maintain a successful color clientele as a hair color specialist.

- To become an education director for a successful salon company.

You may not want to list references on your résumé. In that case, create a separate sheet that lists your references by name, company name, title, address, e-mail address, and phone number. If you choose to have a second sheet, add the following to your résumé: "References available upon request."

Prepare the résumé using a font type that is clear and crisp. Use 14-point size fonts for the heading and 12-point size fonts for the body. Make sure to properly space and tab the text within the document. Run a spell check after you have formatted the entire document. Make sure to proofread your résumé prior to printing and ask someone else to read through it for you.

Choose a fine quality paper and envelope in a neutral color. Make several professional looking copies.

Your Cover Letter

 After completing your résumé, prepare an introductory letter. The purpose of a cover letter is to share a little bit about yourself with a potential employer.

Outline your goals, strengths, and most important personal characteristics. Make sure to request a meeting to discuss opportunities. Finally, indicate when and how you will follow up.

It is important that your letter looks similar to your résumé. Print the letter on the same type of paper you used for the résumé. Use the same typeface and font size. Finally, make sure to sign your letter with a pen. See the example for ideas on how to construct the letter.

Always have your résumé ready and updated. Contact a local printer for design service support. See **Chapter 7** for information about how to utilize your résumé and cover letter.

June 11, 2003

Susan Roberts
Education Director
Beauty Salon and Spa
230 Majestic Road
Los Angeles, CA 90222

Dear Ms. Roberts:

I have recently completed my course of study at PAUL MITCHELL THE SCHOOL.
I am interested in learning more about your salon and the employment opportunities
you may have available. I have enclosed a copy of my résumé for your review. I am an
extremely positive and motivated new professional who would love an opportunity to
work with a successful team in a progressive salon.

My goal is to work within a salon that offers ongoing education. I believe that your salon has many
opportunities for me to grow as a professional. I consider myself service and team-oriented,
enthusiastic, flexible, and open to learning and participating in a variety of salon programs.
I enjoy helping others, and I love what I do. I believe my initial education has helped
me to develop the skills and knowledge necessary to be a successful Salon Professional.

While in school, I developed successful selling and service skills and received recognition
for my retail sales accomplishments. I also participated in a variety of school and industry
events that provided me with wonderful experience and motivated me to be the best I can be.

I am ready to learn and grow with your company and would love the opportunity to meet
with you to discuss opportunities for joining your team. I will contact you next week to schedule
an appointment to discuss your employment process and criteria. If you would like to contact
me or have questions, you may call me at (517) 299-3000. Thank you for your consideration.

Sincerely,

Pamela Miller

Pamela Miller

> Note: You may also include your return address and/or e-mail address.

Your Business Card

It's amazing that a little, tiny piece of paper—your business card—has the power to build your business beyond what you can currently imagine. Your card represents you and is your business identity. It is important that your card's design and layout reflect you as an image and beauty consultant. Keep in mind that you are in the image business, and that your business card needs to show it. Your card should look different from that of other business professionals, such as an accountant's or doctor's business cards. Make it interesting, creative, and functional.

The power of the business card lies in the way it is used. Many schools provide blank cards that you use to promote yourself to potential clients. Purchase a colored pen and neatly write your name on each card. You may also want to print your title as "Future Professional" or "Salon Professional." Get into the habit of always carrying business cards with you and giving them to everyone you meet. Every person is a potential client and is important to your business. The business card is sometimes referred to as a "relationship tool" because it helps you build relationships.

When you begin working in a salon, you will want to work with your employer to get your cards printed as soon as possible. If your salon does not provide business cards, ask the owner's permission to create your own personal business cards that include:

- Your full name
- Your business name or company logo
- Your title
- Your complete business address with zip code
- Your business phone number with area code
- Your business e-mail or Web site address

PAMELA MILLER

1534 ADAMS AVENUE
COSTA MESA, CALIFORNIA 92626
714.546.8786
PAULMITCHELLTHESCHOOL.COM

Business card front

On the back of your business card you may want to include an area for product and service recommendations and future appointment times.

As your business grows, you may want to have a couple of different cards to promote different aspects of your business. For example, you may have a separate card with a different title highlighting your talent as a color specialist, men's grooming specialist, or specialist in long hair.

You may want to have a separate card if you are a part-time educator or a session artist. Make sure to include information that will help you to highlight the services, products, and specialties you offer.

YOUR NEXT SERVICE

DATE: _____ TIME: _____

SHAMPOO: _____

CONDITIONER: _____

STYLE: _____

FINISH: _____

Business card back

YOUR BUSINESS CARD
YOUR IMAGE

❶ Collect other professionals' cards that you like and give your graphic designer ideas for the image you want to project.

Expect to invest a few hundred dollars to have your cards produced and printed.

❷ Use a quality paper that reflects your company's image.

❸ Design your card to look fun and colorful.

❹ Include a logo whenever possible. Logos create brand recognition. The logo should be clean and easily reproducible. A graphic service can help you in creating a logo if one does not exist.

❺ Proofread all copy text prior to printing. It is very costly to reprint.

After you give your approval you are responsible for payment, even with mistakes.

❻ Ask your printer about his quantity pricing. It costs less to print more.

❼ On the back of the card you will want to include a place for product recommendations and appointment times.

The Power of Your Business Card

 The way your card looks is important, but how you use your card is far more important. Use this powerful promotional tool to build your business and professional network of peers. Be business savvy—use your business card to promote additional services and to build referrals. Here's how:

- Give your cards to people in highly visible positions such as food service staff, service providers, hotel service desk personnel, concierge, retail salespeople, sorority or fraternity leaders, models, choir directors, and anyone who is in contact with a lot of people.

- Make certain friends, family members, church members, and anyone you meet professionally or socially has your card. Continually talk about the services you offer and extend an invitation.

- Include your business card in every letter or thank-you card you send.

- Drop your card in promotional "fish bowls" at restaurants and service businesses.

- Place your card on every business bulletin board.

- Mail your card in introductory letters to your local community members.

- Walk around the neighborhood of your salon or school and introduce yourself to every business, invite them to see you, and give them your card.

- Pass your card out at parties, networking meetings, and events.

- Personalize your card with a positive message or your signature.

Cards are powerful when they are placed in the hands of potential clients and associates. Make it a habit to exchange business cards and pass on other professionals' business cards. Remember your card is the single most important marketing tool you own, so get it out of your pocket, wallet, or purse and into the hands of others.

Your Stylebook

Your stylebook is a tool that you will want to start creating shortly after you begin school. A stylebook is a collection of photographs from magazines that you have organized in a photo album or portfolio. It is used during the client consultation. Your stylebook communicates a lot about you and your approach to your craft. You will want to collect a wide variety of beautiful images that appeal to all types of clients, from classic and conservative to street chic and trendy. Depending on your specialty, your stylebook may contain examples of haircuts and styles, beautiful makeup applications, or it may feature hair color.

CREATING A STYLEBOOK

Think of your stylebook as your client's first impression. Make sure it is a beautiful collection of photos in a professional, durable portfolio binder as David Stanko suggests. As you gather images think of the types of services your clients want. Look for a wide range of looks to appeal to a wide range of clients.

To start the process you may want to:

❶ **Look at other professionals' stylebooks to get ideas**.

❷ **Collect beauty, fashion, trade, bridal, and entertainment magazines.**

❸ **Cut out and organize pictures**. Include a variety of images that represent the services you offer.

❹ **Organize sections to feature different services and looks.** The categories may include:

- Short, medium, and long hair styles.

- Classic, trend, or dramatic looks.

- Hair color including brunettes, blondes, reds, dimensional, and special effects.

- Bridal or evening looks.

- Men's styles.

- Various hair textures that highlight the texture and perm services you offer.

- Accessory ideas.

❺ **Tell a story**. Organize your stylebook so that your client can follow along during your consultation.

You may choose current trend looks and include clothing and makeup looks to complement your trend theme.

You may even include small articles or quotes focusing on trends. Your stylebook should tell a story about what is considered beautiful and the current trend.

Your goal as an image consultant is to educate your clients about image and fashion.

Your stylebook is a great educational tool and it helps your clients visualize their new looks.

DAVID STANKO

David Stanko, director of Technical Development for hair color at Redken 5th Avenue NYC, whose work has been seen in top magazines such as Vogue, Cosmopolitan, Glamour, In-Style, *and* Elle, *highly recommends creating a stylebook so that you may express your vision and clearly communicate with your clients. Here are a few of his suggestions:*

I found challenges in expressing my creative vision for my client's hair color in words. I learned early in my career that everyone perceives hair color differently. For example the word "blonde." That one simple word may have one meaning to you and another completely different meaning to your client.

I may have created a beautiful "golden blonde" hair color that I think is beautiful, but my client sees "brassy blonde" tones. Or I may have given her a "creamy light blonde" but all she sees are "platinum or white" tones. If you ever find yourself justifying the color you have created after the service is complete, consider using my portfolio stylebook idea. You can easily create this wonderful consultation tool, which will clarify communication, define hair color terms, and pinpoint a desired shade prior to the application portion of your service.

Go shopping for magazines. Buy everything from mainstream fashion to crazy, runway European fashion magazines. Then invest in a leather bound portfolio, about 11x17 inches should do. Leather is tasteful, professional, and durable. It shows you are serious about your business. Avoid three-ring binders or picture albums with ducks or country motifs. Purchase a box of clear sheet covers to fit the portfolio. They should only open at the top so the photos don't fall out.

> **"'B**londe.' That one simple word may have one meaning to you and a completely different meaning to your client."

Divide your portfolio into four sections: brunette, red, blonde, and men. Cut and insert your collection of pictures. Change your portfolio images seasonally.

A complete hair color portfolio will help you and your client to get on the same page before you begin your service. Now you have a great tool that supports your consultation efforts and clarifies hair color. Gone are the days of confusion when you created "red" and your client saw "mahogany, plum, or fire engine" tones.

Building Your Portfolio

 A portfolio is a pictorial collection of your personal work. Portfolios are another way to establish yourself professionally in the industry and to express your creativity. A portfolio showcases your personal work and accomplishments. Many successful Salon Professionals have developed beautiful portfolios. The process of getting a model and developing an image is also a good way to keep you on "top of your game" and can stimulate your creative energy.

William Williams, a successful session artist located in Los Angeles, has a few suggestions that may help you:

There are so many avenues for building your portfolio. The first place to begin is to decide on the purpose and how you will use your portfolio. For an example, you may want to simply show your personal work to your salon clients, then work with a photographer to create a variety of images that appeal to your clients. Your portfolio may include photos of your work or media mentions.

You may want to build your portfolio to attract media work or editorial recognition. To do this, your book must represent a full spectrum of your work so that you may pursue and attract clients like photographers, designers, magazines, newspapers, television, or video. You may also want to include your work that has been featured in editorial stories.

I first started building my portfolio a very long time ago. It has taken me years to build a book that I am happy with, and I am still building it! You will never finish, as it is always a work in progress.

So be patient and love the process,because it can be fun. Your book will change as your skill develops, the market changes, and fashion changes.

> *Your book will change as your skill develops, the market changes, and fashion changes."*

First things first — Start by contacting agents who specialize in representing session artists and photographers. Ask the agent if there are any of her clients in need of assistants.

Laini Reeves, a successful session artist, says freelance professionals are always looking for knowledgeable, friendly, prompt, and talented assistants. The best way to get started is to build a reputation as a great assistant.

Learn the ropes — Volunteer your time to assist other hair stylists or makeup artists on photo shoots. Experienced professionals can help you to learn what to do and how to handle yourself during photo shoots or backstage during fashion shows. As you learn what to do and learn the rules as you assist others, you will build knowledge and expertise to develop your own images. So do as many photo shoots and volunteer behind the scenes as often as possible.

Do test shoots — A *test shoot* is a photo shoot where everyone works without pay. Test shoots include a photographer, makeup artist, hairdresser, and sometimes an image stylist. The purpose of a test shoot is for the entire group to get great images that each may use to promote her freelance business.

Get connected with lots of different photographers. They are always testing to perfect their ideas and trying to attract new clients. You can do the same. Photographers can also help you develop your business. If they enjoyed working with you and thought your work was good, they will refer you.

Improve your test shoots — The images you produce in test shoots will improve with experience. If you live in an area with few working photographers, contact a local university or art school to connect with photography students.

Observe images in magazines and try to duplicate them for the camera. As time goes on you will learn how to create your own work. You gain creative momentum, which will help you to create a book that you are proud of and that represents your abilities.

"When you are working or assisting on a photo shoot, don't take what anyone says personally...

There is a lot of money involved in photo shoots. Sometimes you may be used and other times you may be canceled at the last minute. That is the nature of the business."

LAINI REEVES

With twenty years in the hairdressing industry, Laini Reeves has established an international reputation for providing inspirational education. Laini holds the prestigious British Hairdressing Award for Afro Hairdresser.

Laini has held the position of education and creative director for Toni & Guy Hairdressing for ten years. She and her team have been winners of the Art Team of the Year for the past ten years.

After joining the Toni & Guy U.S. team as creative director, Laini moved to California to expand the company's education empire. After five exciting years, Laini focused her attention on session work. She currently works in film, fashion magazines, music videos, and advertising. Some of Laini's clients include Nike, Rene Russo, Pamela Anderson, Jessica Biel, Mariah Carey, and China Chow.

Successful freelance artists have the ability to network. We are constantly building contacts, friends, and alliances with a variety of professionals, including models, media, photographers, agents, makeup artists, and other session artists. Most successful artists have a passion for what they do and are continually working to get better and to get their names out.

You may have to start by volunteering your time to assist other hair stylists or makeup artists on photo shoots. Experienced professionals can help you learn what to do and how to handle yourself during shoots. As you learn the ropes and rules by assisting other freelance professionals, you will build expertise and a great reputation.

"Be open to learning, and when working or assisting on a photo shoot, don't take what anyone says personally."

Finally, preparation is very important. As a session artist you must be ready for anything. So invest in your complete professional kit. I have provided suggestions for building your professional kit on Page 94.

The best advice I can give you as you are starting out is to be open to learning, and when working or assisting on a photo shoot, don't take what anyone says personally. There is a lot of money involved in shoots. Sometimes you may be used and other times you may be canceled at the last minute. It is the nature of the business. Stay passionate about building your portfolio and your reputation and you will eventually gain success.

BUILDING YOUR
PORTFOLIO

❶ **Start** participating in photo shoots while you are in school or support salon photo shoots.

❷ **Contact** local photographers or photography students. Volunteer your time and support during test shoots. A test shoot is a photo shoot a photographer does to build his or her portfolio.

❸ **Network** with makeup artists, fashion stylists, and other session hair stylists. Volunteer to assist them whenever you can.

❹ **Find** agents. Ask if they are looking for assistants for their session stylists, makeup artists, or photographers.

Agents are always looking for assistants with strong technical skills to send on photo shoots.

❺ **Do** as many test shoots as possible.

❻ **Study** a variety of print images and try to copy them for the camera.

❼ **Create** a press kit and send your work to magazine editors. A *press kit* is a series of photos with a press release describing your work.

❽ **Continually update** and work on your portfolio. Remember it is a work in progress.

Connecting Tip   #13

Pump Up Your Business With Promotional Tools

- Your business card is your passport to success. Always share it to promote your services.

- Developing a stylebook to show clients is a great way to connect and clarify your vision for their image.

- Building a portfolio helps to expand your client list to include magazines, television, and fashion designers.

SUCCESSFUL

One important way for you to gain recognition and exposure in the beauty industry is through publishing photographs of your work in various beauty and trade magazines. Photo shoots are a great way to get experience working with models, makeup artists, photographers, and fashion stylists.

❶ Gather information — First decide on a look or theme. It can be fun, sexy, playful, classic, or avant-garde. Use fashion and trade magazines for inspiration. Gather ideas from hair shows, fashion shows, television, movies, the Internet, art books, museums, model schools, and on the street. Create a collage of ideas.

❷ Find your model — There are two ways to approach your model search. You may find a model that inspires you to do a certain look, or you may find a look and then search for the perfect model.

Models can be recruited from your clients, class-mates, friends, co-workers, modeling agencies or schools, college campuses, high schools, and malls. Find a model that is comfortable in front of a camera. Some of the most beautiful people can be very unphotogenic.

Test shots with a Polaroid camera may help. Check out the model's face shape, bone structure, body type, skin, facial features, and hands. Make sure your model has healthy, shiny, beautiful hair.

❸ Doing the "do" — Magazine editors look for images that are creative, unique, beautiful, interesting, new, news-worthy, classic, or elegant. Hair must be shiny and healthy. Avoid overworking the hair. The camera magnifies imperfections, so make sure your work is flawless. Look through the lens often to check details. The haircut, color, perm, relaxer, and style must be well-executed. Fix stray hairs. Hair should be smooth. Be careful not to overuse product. Comb the hair for a silk finish.

❹ Perfect makeup — Think of makeup as an integral accessory. It pulls the whole look together and can easily enhance or detract from the hair style.

When choosing the style of makeup, it is important to have a clear vision of the desired outcome. Maintain a timeless look by keeping makeup classic and subtle, like the makeup you would see in old Hollywood photographs.

For a more current look, follow the latest trends in placement and color.

For best results:

- Choose a model with clear skin.

- Groom his or her eyebrows, trim, tweeze, and color if necessary.

- Prepare the skin by applying moisturizer. This helps in blending foundation.

- Apply foundation or base to even out the complexion. As a general rule keep some warmth in the base.

PHOTO SHOOTS

- You may want to go one or two shades darker than the skin tone. Make sure the skin tone on the face is not dramatically different from the neck or body.

- Use body makeup with a large sponge to even out the skin tone on all exposed skin.

- Blend, blend, and keep on blending. Photographs accentuate imperfections and improper product applications.

- Neutralize negative tones, like dark circles, red overtones, or blemishes with color correctors or concealers.

- Blend eye shadow until it blends in and disappears into the skin color.

- Evenly apply lip color, make sure that the lips appear balanced, and avoid drooping corners.

- Even out complexion and enhance coloring of male models. Makeup should not appear to be obvious.

- Be aware of the depth and intensity of the color you are using if you will be shooting black and white photography.

- There are many ways to learn the art of makeup:

  Attend professional makeup schools, assist a professional makeup artist, and self-direct your learning with books by professional makeup artists like: François Nars, Sam Fine, Kevyn Aucoin, Serge Lutens, and Richard Corson, just to name a few.

❺ **Clothing —**
Your model's wardrobe can greatly effect the overall look and feel of the finished photograph.

Choose clothing that is clean, current, classic, and elegant. Clothing should not be frayed and must be wrinkle-free and properly fitted. Simple designer clothes are always a good and safe choice.

You may also select casual, trendy, or retro clothing if it enhances the overall look of the model. Clothing should never distract from the overall look.

- Avoid unnecessary and inappropriate bare skin.

- Use discretion with glasses or sunglasses.

- Avoid clothing made from animal products like fur, feathers, suede, or leather.

- Avoid inappropriate props like cigarettes or liquor.

Choose subtle and properly coordinated jewelry and accessories. Remember you are trying to create an overall beautiful look that emphasizes the beauty of your model.

❻ **Photographer —**
Work with a professional. Look for a fashion photographer, rather than a portrait photographer. Or find an up-and-coming photography student eager to experiment and work with you.

Ask to review the photographer's portfolio. If you are paying a professional, make sure to see a variety of close-ups that demonstrate the ability to capture the beauty and essence of the subjects.

Make sure the photographer knows how to use lights to enhance the hair and makeup.

BUILD YOUR
PROFESSIONAL KIT

Laini Reeves, a successful freelance session artist located in Los Angeles, recommends that you create a photo shoot kit filled with the following "must haves":

- Two ultra light blow-dryers.

- All sizes of curling irons including small, medium, medium/large, and large.

- Three sizes of flat irons including mini, ceramic, and jumbo.

- One diffuser.

- Hot rollers and Velcro rollers.

- Every size of round brush including soft and metal bristles.

- Two soft bristle brushes and two half-round brushes.

- A variety of combs.

- A variety of scissors, razors, and carving combs.

- A variety of clips, binders, hair accessories, and pins in all colors.

- Wefts of hair in all colors including black, brown, dark brown, blonde, and red.

- Wigs in a variety of colors and lengths. They do not have to be expensive if you know how to style wigs.

Laini recommends researching and testing equipment and products to find your favorites. Also, learn how to use what you have. The key is to be prepared prior to arriving at a photo shoot.

Tools of the Trade

A craftsman is only as good as his tools. These are words to live by in an industry built on innovation and technique. You will want to invest a portion of your income each year in developing and maintaining your tools.

Build a relationship with a scissors manufacturer or vendor — Many professionals buy their tools directly from the manufacturer. They can also help you service and maintain your scissors.

Shop at trade shows to learn more about what's available — However, be careful in making a purchase. You want to buy from someone who will be around to service your tools. Talk to other professionals—tools are a major investment. Learn from others which tools they use most often and which brands they like the best.

Learn how to take care — Learn how to properly take care of and maintain your tools. Have your equipment serviced and your scissors sharpened by the scissors manufacturer or a very reputable dealer. The sharpening process is very critical and, if done improperly, can ruin an expensive tool.

Buy what you like — Take the recommendation of an expert, but in the end buy what is most comfortable for you. Always buy quality.

Connecting Tip   #14

Your Gear

As a professional and craftsman you must invest in and care for a variety of quality tools.

Create and maintain a professional kit. Build a relationship with quality vendors and manufacturers. Stay on top of trends and innovations and make informed buying decisions.

GAME PLAN

BUILD

In this chapter you learned about the tools of your trade. Let's create the fourth step of your game plan. Make a commitment to develop your tool kit.
Write your commitment here.

REFLECT

Think about what fears or obstacles may interfere with keeping your commitment. ***Write them here.***

TAKE ACTION

PROMOTE

Invest in a professional-looking business card. Use it at all times to build relationships and your clientele.

CREATE

Create a professional stylebook that reflects the type of services you can offer.

SHOOT

Participate in photo shoots while you are in school. Create a professional portfolio made from photos of your work.

INVEST

Invest in quality tools and develop a complete tool kit that you maintain for your profession.

"Business is like theater. Successful people give award-winning performances."

PAUL MITCHELL THE SCHOOL

A C T

Chapter 5

My Clients

Lights! Camera! Action! Imagine that you were starring in a blockbuster Hollywood movie. You are playing the part of an expert image professional. Your character is the best service and retail professional in the world. Your wardrobe is spectacular. Your script is perfect. The stage is set, and all of your co-stars are ready with their parts.

You deliver lines with passion and confidence. Both the critics and audience hail your award-winning performance. Believe it or not, you already are the star performer in your client's salon experience. Because of you, your clients look great and feel wonderful.

The salon industry is much like show business. Your salon is your stage. You have a role to play that follows a script. Your teammates are fellow actors and your clients are your audience and hopefully your fan club. Your income and success are based on your performance. It's all up to you.

In this chapter you will learn to set the stage, play the part, and create an experience your clients will love. Your award-winning performance will make you a successful and prosperous professional.

Attracting and connecting with clients

Think about:

- What does unbelievable client service look and feel like?

- What is my new role?

- What steps should I follow to create success?

- How can I connect with my clients?

- What will make me unique as a professional?

Learn about:

- Business is like theater.

- Setting the stage.

- Preparing for your role.

- Your performance.

Learn from:

- John and Melissa Ryan

- Kate Troc

Business Is Like Theater

In the past decade, the beauty industry has become increasingly more sophisticated and focused on creating successful business practices. As salons transform, so must the traditional roles of salon owner, manager, receptionist, hairdresser, and spa professional.

Services are now considered experiences, much like the experience of attending a play. You and your team must become producers, directors, choreographers, and actors all playing to an audience of clients. The more successfully you and your team members play your roles, the better the audience's experience. The effect of a haircut lasts a few weeks, but you can give clients an experience they will remember much longer. Learn to create the ultimate service experience by paying attention to what your audience wants and needs.

Setting the Stage

One of the most successful businesses today is Starbucks. The company has taken a very simple product, a cup of coffee, and transformed it into an experience. Coffee costs very little, yet they can charge a premium price. Why? Because of the experience they offer.

Starbucks has employed well-trained, friendly team members who consistently provide great service and beverages. They pay attention to what people want most—a place to hang out. They have set the stage and they attract customers by the hundreds of thousands. Your salon or school has the same potential and opportunity to attract great clients.

Think about your salon or school's service environment. Is it a beautiful, clean, comfortable, and friendly place to visit? Do your clients look and feel better when they leave? Would they pay a premium price for the experience?

5 Senses Program

By creating an environment and experience that appeals to your client's senses and preferences, you can become just like Starbucks—always attracting and retaining ideal clients. The 5 Senses Program is a guide for creating an unbelievable client experience and will help you set the stage.

1 **Visual** — Clean up the mess! Clients love a clean place to come and relax. Your clients may have their cars detailed often and employ a cleaning person. They may love to shop at Nordstrom's. Your goal is to create an environment that is cleaner than your client's home and as attractive as Nordstrom's. Arrange your tools and products in an appealing and organized manner. Decide which products you are using and which you want to promote for purchase.

Create interesting things for clients to look at. Hang current fashion images around the salon. Provide an updated stylebook, including pictures of your own work. Set out upbeat fashion, fitness, or health magazines.

Finally, look the part. Imagine if you went to see *Phantom of the Opera* and the evening you attended the lead actor decided he didn't want to wear his costume or makeup. One of the most important things you can do to appeal to your client's visual senses is to look the part of a successful image professional. They come to you for beauty and image advice and expect you to look the part.

2 **Smell** — The sense of smell is strongly tied to memory. If you want your client to remember you and her experience, use products with fragrances your client loves. If a client likes the way a product smells, it gives you an opportunity to point out the benefits of the products and encourage a purchase. When your client returns home and uses the products, she is likely to remember her great service experience. Think of hair care, skin care, and makeup products as wonderful reminders for your client to return to you.

> " The 5 Senses Program is a guide for creating an unbelievable client experience and will help you set the stage."

Sweet smell of freshness — Ensure good air quality in the school or salon.

- Remove offensive odors by misting the air, running an air purifier, or burning candles.
- Refrain from smoking between clients. Nonsmokers are especially sensitive to the smell of cigarettes.
- Make sure your breath is fresh and pleasant. Take a toothbrush and toothpaste to work and use mints.
- Wear a light fragrance. Use deodorant and make sure your clothes smell fresh.

There are very few professions where touch is allowed. Take this unique opportunity to build a bond with your client that may last for years."

3 Taste — Do you offer refreshments to your clients? If so, great! What you serve is as important as how you serve it.

- Serve only fine quality coffee or teas, purified water, or any other drink that is refreshing and tasteful.
- Offer gourmet drinks in clean mugs and spot-free glasses. Avoid styrofoam.
- Serve lemonade or iced tea with real ice cubes and lemon wedges.
- Make sure the serving area is clean.
- Carry your clients' drinks back to your station for them.
- Offer refills and discard their glasses or cups when they are finished.

4 Touch — Client surveys have shown that what they liked best about their visits to the salon was the wonderful massage at the shampoo bowl, manicure station, or during the facial. Invite your client to relax as you gently massage and release her tension and prepare her for an enjoyable service.

- During a shampoo, provide an extra long head massage.
- During a chemical service, surprise your client with a hand massage using a special lotion with her favorite fragrance.
- During a facial, incorporate a neck and shoulder massage, or a hand and arm massage.
- During body treatments, offer a foot massage.

There are very few professions where touch is allowed. Take this unique opportunity to build a bond with your client that may last for years.

Hearing — Your clients' experiences are profoundly shaped by what they hear. The music and conversation around them will put them in a state of relaxation or irritation. Clients will have a wide variety of musical tastes, but national surveys reveal that the majority of clients prefer light jazz music to any other. This means that you may have to endure listening to music that does not fit your taste. Remember that your role as an actor is to provide a great experience for your client.

Motivate yourself — You can consistently meet your client's needs by motivating yourself to do what your client loves, even if it isn't your most favorite thing to do.

Rehearsal

In the past decade there has been a decline in customer service standards. As a customer, you may have grown accustomed to unenthusiastic service providers and disappointing service experiences. Mediocre service has become common, while great service is rare.

When you suffer through a bad service experience, you probably let everyone know so they don't get the same bad service. When you have exceptionally good service, you may also tell everyone about it. Studies have shown that the most effective way to attract new clients is from the recommendations of your loyal clients. A great experience can motivate and inspire your clients to tell everyone they know.

Connecting Tip   #16

5 Senses Program

You create an unbelievable client experience by paying attention to details and implementing the 5 Senses Program.

- Appeal to your clients visually.
- Appeal to your client's sense of smell.
- Appeal to your client's sense of taste.
- Appeal to your client's sense of touch.
- Appeal to your client's sense of hearing.

It's simple, providing exceptional service is very good for your business and is the best way to build long-term relationships with loyal clients. Always give your best performance and think of your client's recommendation as a standing ovation.

Learn Your Lines

 The conversation that you have with your client is clearly one of the most important aspects of her visit and experience.

Words are amazing. Once you say them, they can have a great effect on your client's perception of you. The following is a list of "old script" you want to eliminate and "new script" you will want to learn and use when speaking with your clients. The new words will make you appear knowledgeable and service-oriented.

Your Old Script	Your New Script
Mistake	Discovery
Client	Guest
Staff	Associates
Teacher/instructor	Learning Leader
Student	Future Professional
Stylist	Salon Professional
Customer	Guest
Hi/hey/hello	Good morning/afternoon/evening
Hi	Welcome
Can I help you?	How may I assist you?
Book an appointment	Reserve time
Running late	A bit behind schedule
Okay/sure thing	Certainly
You're welcome/no problem	It's my pleasure
Good idea	Excellent choice
Sorry about that	Please forgive me or I apologize
I'll take care of it	I will personally see to it
Raise prices	Adjust prices
Cost	Investment
Shampoo bowl	Cleansing area
Station	Design area
Problem	Challenge
Rules or policies	Guidelines

Playing the Role of a Successful Professional

 The goal of defining your role is to help you relate to clients who can afford and are willing to pay a premium price for your services. Within the industry there are successful professionals who have learned to speak and act in ways that help them build a large clientele. They are the star performers of the beauty industry. The way to become a star performer is to observe the qualities of other star performers and then create similar star qualities within you.

Star qualities — Star qualities are the things that you do to build long-term relationships with your guests and team. Your role as a successful image consultant can be learned. The Star Quality Checklist will provide you ideas about how to think, communicate, and act like a successful professional. See Page 106.

Communicate Success

Your success is based on your technical skills, your verbal communication, and your nonverbal communication. Some of the most technically accomplished professionals are not always the ones with the biggest clientele. Some very talented professionals tend to neglect the communication side of the profession. Would you rather be a starving "artist" or a wealthy Salon Professional with a loyal clientele? If you chose a wealthy Salon Professional, then become a master communicator.

Your ability to communicate both verbally and nonverbally is the most important aspect of playing your role. Your overall success is based:

- 15 percent on your technical skills
- 30 percent on your verbal communication skills
- 55 percent on your nonverbal communication skills

Your appearance, image, attitude, and self-esteem are critical to your success and your business. Act the part. Your role as a professional may be very different from the role you play at home with family or friends. Create a strategy to improve. Think of all of the things you will check for improvement in the Star Quality Checklist and brainstorm ways you can learn and develop.

Act the part. Your role as a professional may be very different from the role you play at home with family or friends."

Your ability to communicate both verbally and nonverbally is the most important aspect of playing your role."

Star Quality Checklist

Put a star by the "star qualities" you already possess and put a check next to those qualities you need to improve.

Your Verbal Communication
The way you speak can greatly affect your relationship with your guests.

☒ You speak clearly in a volume appropriate to the environment.
☒ You sound enthusiastic and excited about the products and services you offer.
✓ You explain technical jargon.
✓ You ask questions to determine what your guest wants and prefers.
☒ You refrain from using slang or profanity.
☒ You are always helping your guest to relax.
✓ You educate and provide a thorough consultation with every service.
☒ You follow the 10 Opportunities during the service.
☒ You complete each service using the 2-Minute Plan.
✓ You call to follow up or send a thank-you note.

Your Nonverbal Communication
Your actions always speak louder than your words.

☒ You give great eye contact to your guests and smile frequently.
☒ You follow your team's image and dress guidelines.
☒ Your makeup, hair, and skin reflect current trends and beauty standards.
✓ You shake hands with your guest when you meet. Your handshake is firm, not overpowering.
✓ You place your hands on your guest's shoulders during the consultation.
✓ You give a relaxing massage during every service.
✓ You hold the product you are recommending and then hand it to your guest as you talk about it.
☒ You watch your guests' body language and make adjustments to ensure they are comfortable and happy.

Your Attitudes and Characteristics
Your professional personality can help you to attract success, happiness, and wealth.

☒ You are positive and refrain from criticisms, negativity, gossip, and unproductive behavior.
☒ You focus on what is working. You look for solutions to improve what isn't working.
☒ You are organized and clean.
☒ You are friendly and interested in other people.
☒ You love to learn new things and are open-minded.
✓ You are informed about the latest products, service techniques, fashion, and beauty trends.
☒ You give back to your team and help others whenever you can.
☒ You follow guidelines and support your leaders.
☒ You lead a balanced and moderate lifestyle.
☒ You persistently work toward your goals.

Your Performance

Each day you are in the salon or school you are on stage and performing your role. Thus far in this chapter you have studied and prepared for your role. Now you should be ready to deliver a great performance. There are service opportunities at each step of the salon experience. Learn to perform well during every phase of your guest's salon visit.

First Impressions

- **The phone call**
- **Guest welcome**
- **Your greeting**

Ideal Guest Experience

- **Consultation**
- **Service experience**
- **Service follow-up**

First Impressions

You and your team send messages to your guests all of the time. How you answer the phone, welcome guests, and greet everyone is critical to building long-term relationships. During the first moments of every guest's visit, she is gathering information and making assessments about you and you are making a first impression. Learn how you and your team can connect and set the tone for creating a wonderful guest experience.

The secret to a great performance is paying attention and taking advantage of the opportunities you have to connect with your guests before, during, and after their visits. You and your team have the ability to build or block a great service experience for your guests.

Connecting Tip   #17

Be a Star

Guests are attracted or repelled by the way you communicate and act. Develop the attitude and characteristics of a successful image consultant, and you will automatically attract a large audience.

The Phone Call

The relationship your team establishes with your guest begins with the initial phone call. Follow simple phone etiquette when answering the phone. These tips will help you make a great first impression. Take time to review the following checklist and share ideas on how to improve with your team members and leaders. It is everyone's responsibility to assist in developing a positive first impression.

The Phone Call Checklist

☐ Answer the phone within three rings.

☐ Smile. Your guest can tell if you are smiling.

☐ Use a pleasant and friendly voice.

☐ Say, "Thank you for calling (salon name), this is (identify yourself by your first name). How may I assist you?"

☐ Wait until the caller responds. Then ask permission to put her on hold or continue helping her.

☐ Ask questions that help and direct the caller. For example, "What day of the week and time of day is best for you?" and "What type of service would you like to schedule?"

☐ Provide suggestions for scheduling additional services. For example, "Can we schedule a manicure as well?" or "We are running an introductory offer on our new massage service. Would you like to schedule a half hour before your hair appointment?"

☐ Provide accurate information. Do not guess. Give specific prices, products, services, or directions. If you aren't sure, ask to put the guest on hold while you check.

☐ Confirm scheduled appointments. Clarify any directions or arrangements.

☐ Thank the person for calling.

Phone Call Service Blockers

■ Rushing through the greeting, sounding like *"Thankyouforcallingcarelesssalonpleasehold."* Or saying, "Please hold" and then cutting the caller off.

■ Making comments to others while your caller is trying to ask a question or give you information. Rushing the caller off the phone to get back to your personal call or movie magazine.

■ Guessing at information or muffling the phone while you ask a question of a passing team member.

■ Expecting the caller to remember all of the details of what you said.

■ Saying, "OK, bye." Then hanging up while the caller is trying to say goodbye or asking one last question.

The Guest Welcome

The first minutes of the guest's visit are critical to setting the stage for the remainder of her experience. As guests enter they may feel excited, nervous, tired, stressed out, or intimidated. No matter how wonderful your relationship is with your guests, it can be affected by how they are treated by others within the salon or school. If guests are not comfortable from the beginning to the end of the entire visit, they will be less likely to return.

You may not be able to change what other students or team members do, but you can be an excellent service role model. We suggest that you make it your business to help everyone on your team to provide great guest services. Create awareness of the importance of working together to build a warm and inviting service environment.

Create awareness of the importance of working together to build a warm and inviting service environment."

The Guest Welcome Checklist

- [ ] Welcome all guests moments after they enter the salon or school.

- [ ] Say, "Good (morning/afternoon/evening). Welcome to (salon/school name). How may I assist you today?" Use the guest's name if you know it.

- [ ] If you are busy, simply look up and acknowledge the guest and say, "Welcome, I will be with you as soon as I can." An immediate acknowledgment is very important.

- [ ] Smile and welcome all guests entering the facility, no matter what you are doing and no matter if they are your guests or not.

- [ ] If you notice guests waiting without assistance, acknowledge them and help them immediately, or let them know that you will get someone to help them.

Service Blockers to the Welcome

- Instructing guests to "wait" in the guest waiting area.
- Making personal calls, reading, or visiting with team members.
- Being M.I.A. (missing in action) when guests are looking at products.
- Looking mentally "out to lunch" as guests pass.
- Serving day-old coffee or warm iced tea.
- Letting guests aimlessly wander through the salon as they desperately look for the restroom or changing area.
- Allowing guests to wait and wait and wait and wait with no information.
- Expecting guests to sit in a dirty or smelly environment while listening to personal chatter between team members that competes with the irritating music being played by the receptionist.

Your Greeting

Your guest is now seated comfortably in the seating area, sipping a refreshing cup of coffee or tea and ready for your performance. Here is an easy greeting checklist to connect with your guest at the beginning of every service visit.

Remember the first few minutes with your guests are extremely important. Help them to feel comfortable and able to trust that you will help them look and feel more beautiful.

The Greeting Checklist

- [ ] Walk toward the guest, smile, make eye contact, and hold out your hand.

- [ ] Say, "Hello, (guest's name), nice to see you again," or "Welcome, it's a pleasure to meet you."

- [ ] Pause and let the guest respond.

- [ ] Invite the guest to your work area, changing area, or consultation area. Walk together toward your destination.

- [ ] Offer to refill refreshments.

- [ ] Assist and guide the guest at all times. Provide a tour for new guests.

Greeting Blockers

- Looking like you just swallowed a bitter pill as you roll your eyes with your hands on your hips.

- Offering the "dead fish" handshake.

- Waving the guest back to your station.

- Saying, "Follow me," then walking toward your station without looking back.

- Letting guests fumble with empty glasses or wonder if they could possibly have more.

- Saying, "Take a seat," as you tidy your station.

- Rushing guests past a sea of busy, frazzled, crabby team members.

Create the Ideal Guest Experience

Create the ideal guest experience by consistently following the 10 Opportunities and using the 2-Minute Plan. Your guests look to you as a source of information and support. These are your scripts for serving them.

Start by reading the overview of the 10 Opportunities. Next, learn how to integrate these steps into each aspect of the service experience you offer your guests.

10 Opportunities

Steps for creating the ideal service experience

During the Consultation

1. Ask, "What challenges are you having with your hair?"

2. Answer the challenge by recommending the appropriate products and services.

3. Retrieve the product off the retail shelf, and place it in your guest's hand during the service.

During the Shampoo

4. Give your guest a wonderful massage while shampooing.

5. Explain and educate your guest about the recommended shampoo and conditioner.

6. Place the appropriate shampoo and conditioner bottles in your guest's hand to carry to your station.

During the Service

7. Continue talking professionally as you educate your guest about her individual beauty needs and how your products will enhance the look you are creating with your service.

8. Before styling your guest's hair, allow her to see, touch, smell, and use the finishing products before you apply them to the hair.

9. After styling, spend a few minutes with your guest explaining how the various products you used have solved the challenges. Again, make sure the product is in her hand as you discuss it.

10. Follow all of the steps of the 2-Minute Plan. *See Page 121.*

The service experience is filled with opportunities to connect with your guests. One of the most important ways you can service your guests is to recommend additional services they may need and create a home care plan that they can follow between visits. The more successfully your guest can maintain what you have created, the more likely she is to return and refer others.

The Guest Consultation

The goal of the guest consultation is to identify your guest's vision for her skin, makeup, or hair and to create a game plan of how to create a look that she will love. It is your role as the skilled and knowledgeable service professional to guide your guest through the decision-making process. Guests won't always know what they want or need. They need you to help them to figure that out.

During the consultation, you also have the opportunity to gain a guest's trust and to help her relax. The best way to get your guest to trust and like you is to show that you are interested in helping her. You can learn about your guest and build her trust when you:

- Connect by asking a lot of questions to uncover her vision of her image.

- Connect by listening to what she says and observing her body language.

If you are distracted or rushing through the consultation you may miss important clues and information that could lead to your guest's disappointment in the final outcome.

Connect by asking questions. There is an art to questioning. Open-ended questions usually bring better, more detailed responses. Ask open-ended questions to gather information about what the guest likes and dislikes. Confirm with closed questions before you move forward.

Guests won't always know what they want or need. They need you to help them to figure that out."

Open-Ended Questions

Open-ended questions are phrased so that the person answering must provide more than a yes or no answer.

These questions begin with:

- Who
- What
- Where
- Why
- When
- How

For example, "What challenges have you been having with your hair, skin, and makeup?"

Closed-Ended Questions

Closed-ended questions confirm what your guest wants and are usually answered with a yes or no statement.

They tend to begin with:

- Would
- Do
- Did
- Could
- May
- Can

For example, "Just to confirm, did you say you would like your hair about chin length?"

Connect by Listening and Observing

Asking questions is critical to gathering information. However, as you ask questions make sure you are listening with a quiet mind. Listening means that you are hearing with the intent to understand what the guest is saying. To improve your listening skills:

Focus — Look into your guest's eyes and focus on what she is saying.

Confirm — Confirm what you heard by rephrasing the questions or her responses. If you do not understand, rephrase your question. Continue to ask questions until you are certain you understand your client's needs.

> *Listening means that you are hearing with the intent to understand what the guest is saying."*

Look for clues – Finally, watch your guest's body language. Her body language will tell you when she is comfortable or in discomfort. Your guest's facial expressions and body movements are also clues to how comfortable she is, so look for signs of comfort and discomfort throughout the service.

Signs of Comfort

Smiling

Relaxed breathing

Relaxing arms and legs

Dropping shoulders

Laughing, talking, and asking questions

Signs of Discomfort

Frowning, tightening face or furrowing brow

Deep sighing or fast breathing

Crossing arms or legs or fidgeting

Holding shoulders up around the neck

Avoiding eye contact, becoming quiet or withdrawn, or crying

When your guest is in discomfort, stop and adjust what you are doing. Take control of the situation immediately by asking more questions. Let your guest know that you will only do what he or she is comfortable with you doing.

Get Help and Be Open

If you are a Future Professional working in a school or a new stylist, you will want to summarize a description of what your guests desires and discuss it with your Learning Leader or a senior stylist. Make sure to ask for help and be open to suggestions and ideas on how best to perform the service.

Some Additional Tips for Successful Consultations:
- Show pictures.
- Show hair color swatches.
- Do a swatch test (for perms or colors).
- Lift the hair into place.
- Ask for a second opinion.

Consultation
Checklist

**Here are some simple steps for uncovering challenges
and opportunities to help guests look and feel better.**

☐ **Ask questions** — Gather information and gain an understanding of your guests' challenges and goals. The following is a list of effective questions to ask during a consultation:

- **What** challenges have you been having with your hair, skin, or makeup?
- **How** much time do you like to spend getting ready in the morning?
- **When** was your last service?
- **What** types of services (color/perm) have you had in the past six months?
- **What** products are you currently using on your hair or skin? Before we move forward, does this sound like a product you would like?

☐ **Listen** — Show your willingness to listen by waiting for your guest's responses without interrupting. She will share her challenges, which are your opportunities to help her.

☐ **Answer your guest's challenges with recommendations** — Always confirm what you heard your guest say. Then recommend the appropriate products and services to solve her challenges.

☐ **Retrieve the product off the retail shelf and place it in your guest's hand** — Why would you want to put the products in their hands? How do you sell a puppy? When your guest touches and feels the products, they will sell themselves.

☐ **Make your service and product recommendations** — Complete the consultation with a service and product recommendation. Take time to explain what you will do during the service and begin your product recommendations for home care based on what you have learned so far. Share your recommendation in two parts:

Say *"Based on your description of what you would like to achieve, I recommend we do (describe an overview of the service). How does our plan sound?"*

Wait for your guest's response and look for her comfort level.

Say *"I also recommend (list shampoo and conditioner). I'll use them during your shampoo and scalp massage. At the end of our service, I will help you create a home care plan to maintain your new look."*

Once again listen and wait for a response. Look into her eyes as she speaks to you and observe her facial expression. Ensure that she feels comfortable with moving forward.

MELISSA

John and Melissa Ryan own Festoon Salon. Their salon has been open for 13 years in Berkeley, California, and they recently opened Festoon S.F. in San Francisco, California. Their salons are highly profitable, with the San Francisco salon generating $1 million the first year in business. Retail sales make up an amazing 30 percent of total income.

We opened Festoon Salon with the hopes of creating a salon atmosphere where our team could grow, prosper, be challenged, and enjoy a beautiful environment. Unfortunately, in the beginning the salon didn't make any money, even though everyone was busy and booked in advance. There came a point where we couldn't continue to allow our business to stay open without it being profitable.

We tried to figure out why we didn't meet our goals. We realized that in order for Festoon to be successful, there had to be a supportive relationship between our business and our artistry. We created the F-Team to develop a successful strategy. It was created with the following beliefs:

- Everyone must work together toward a common goal.
- When our goals are reached, then everyone wins.
- If the goals are not accomplished, then the whole team falls short.
- When everyone participates, it provides support and motivation for the team to succeed.
- In order to achieve success, everyone must have full clientele, strong retail numbers, and the motivation to grow.

Senior team members guide and support junior team members through technical and creative skills. Our guests feel free to experience services with many of our stylists. We created scripts to communicate, recommend, and service our guests.

& JOHN RYAN

"**A**lways complete the service by following up and reviewing what you recommended…"

Start with a recommendation. Who said you had to make your recommendations at the end of the service? Start the service with an initial product and service recommendation right after you have completed the consultation.

Make retail part of the service. Consider the products you retail as an extension of the service you provide within the salon. Retail helps the bottom line. We believe that our team must focus equal amounts of time on recommending and providing home care products and additional services and on performing haircuts. In today's market, a salon earns a profit margin of only about seven percent from each haircut, whereas the profit from retail is approximately 35 to 40 percent. It makes more sense to focus on retailing.

End with a recommendation. Always complete the service by following up and reviewing what you recommended and making future service and product recommendations. Your professional recommendation is really important to your guests. If they are unable to afford the products during the current service, they will surely make a purchase during the next service. Know your numbers. Learn about the financial and productivity side of the business. You will see a pattern of growth and be able to identify areas to improve. As you learn your numbers, you will find that you become motivated to achieve success.

To learn more about Festoon Salon's training program, visit their Web site at www.festoonsalon.com.

The Guest Service Experience

A guest service is divided into two segments:
- **The Shampoo**
- **The Service**

Remember your goal is to create an experience, not just service your guest. Think in terms of the services you provide from your guest's perspective.

Become guest-focused — Put yourself in your guest's shoes and ask, "What would I like to experience?" Each of your guests is unique. Your goal is to provide them with an experience that meets their specific expectations, preferences, and needs.

Think of the service in terms of what the guest will experience, rather than what you will do. This will help you to develop sensitivity to your guest's unique needs and in turn build a long-term relationship.

Provide pleasant surprises — Great service experiences are filled with pleasant surprises that help guests enjoy and relax while they allow you to do your magic. Those added touches make your guest feel like she is on center stage. Pamper, listen, recommend, and solve her challenges. The more you can solve challenges, the more connected and loyal she will become.

> Studies have shown that when new guests purchase three products, there is a 90 percent chance they will return to your salon a second time.
>
> Guest purchases two products – 60 percent chance of a return visit.
>
> Guest purchases one product – 30 percent chance of a return visit.
>
> Guest purchases no products – 10 percent chance of a return visit.

The Shampoo

Guest surveys have shown that what guests liked best about their visits to the salon was the wonderful massage at the shampoo bowl, manicure station, or during the facial. In contrast, Salon Professional surveys have revealed that what Salon Professionals hate most about performing a service was doing the massage. This is interesting because even though most professionals know their guests love the massage during the service, only one in 10 can honestly say they provide a wonderful massage to every guest at each visit.

Now this is a no-brainer. If your guest's favorite part of the service is the scalp massage during the shampoo, then just do it. Make it your favorite part. When you give, you will definitely receive. Your guests will recognize the difference and reward you accordingly.

The Shampoo Checklist

☐ Always give your guest a wonderful massage during every service.

Make certain to:

- Invite her to take a couple of deep breaths and relax.
- Lower your voice and allow her to let go of any stress.
- Massage her scalp, neck, and shoulders.
- Ask if the massage pressure is okay.
- Use warm water and gently rinse.
- Surprise her with a warm towel treatment and allow her to relax for a few moments longer.
- Squeeze water out of the hair. Towel dry. Do not allow the hair to drip.
- Apply a fresh dry towel.
- Blot dry your guest's forehead, neck, and ears.
- Remove the wet towel before returning to your station.
- Comb the hair out with a wide comb or paddle brush.

☐ Educate your guest about the shampoo and conditioner you recommend for her. You may begin by asking your guest how her shampoo service was. After her response, take time to explain the benefits of and reasons you chose to use the specific shampoo and conditioner during the service.

☐ If you haven't already, put the appropriate shampoo and conditioner bottles into your guest's hand. Allow your guest to smell and experience the product. You may help your guest carry the products to the station.

The Service

Make your primary goal to build a friendly professional relationship with your guests. Be friendly, but remember they are not your friends. Your friends don't pay you for your services. Keep conversations focused on your guests' favorite topic—them. Avoid conversation topics like religion, politics, and your personal life.

Rather than spending time on small talk, show your guest what you are using, how to apply products, and how to blow-dry or style her hair. Teach her how to recreate what you have created for her. The purpose of the service is to make her beautiful; but it is also to help her to recreate her look after she leaves, by educating her on what to do and what to use.

The Service Checklist

☐ **Continue to talk professionally as you educate your guest about her individual beauty needs.**

Educate yourself on what products will enhance the look you are creating.

- Look for opportunities to solve her challenges.
- Focus attention on creating her experience.
- Offer solutions.
- Listen to her and observe how she is responding.
- Make adjustments as needed to make sure she feels completely pampered, relaxed, and informed.

☐ **Before styling, allow your guest to see, touch, smell, and use the finishing products before you apply them to her hair.**

- Share tips on how to style and finish her hair during the styling portion of the service.
- Show her how to hold the brush and blow-dryer or iron.

☐ **After styling, spend a few minutes explaining how the various products you used have solved the challenges.**

- Again make sure the product is in her hands.
- Provide her with a styling tip list.
- Provide care directions for hair color and perms.
- Share information about tools and products.

☐ **Follow all of the steps in the 2-Minute Plan.**

Connecting Tip   #18

10 Opportunities

Create the ultimate guest experience by following the 10 Opportunities steps during the consultation, shampoo, and throughout the entire service.

A Service Completion Process

The 2-Minute Plan is a service completion process that when consistently performed at the end of each service, will ensure successful completion to a great service experience. The purpose of the 2-Minute Plan is to help you focus on what is most important. It's a plan of success for retail and guest retention.

2-Minute Plan

To begin immediately after the service is complete.

1. **Wait to clean your station.**
   Your time with your guest is important.
   Clean your station when your guest has left.

2. **Escort your guest to the reception area.**
   Walk with your guest.

3. **Introduce your guest to the receptionist.**
   An introduction allows the receptionist to support you in completing the service and retail purchase transaction. The receptionist may also support your work by complimenting the guest on her new look.

4. **Pull products and focus on solutions.**
   Place the products in her hands and say, "These are the products I used on you today. I recommend that you use them to maintain your look. The receptionist can write them up for you."

5. **Reserve a future service time.**
   Reserve her next service time or at least recommend future services and times to return. Try to schedule other types of services within the next couple of days. Say, "Let's schedule you to return for that additional service we discussed."

6. **Give your guest your business card.**
   Write your product and future service recommendations on the back of your card. Document the time and date of the next scheduled appointment.

2-Minute Plan (continued on next page)

7. **Give your guest five to 10 business cards.**
   Say, "Would you please share my cards with your friends who might benefit from my services?"

8. **Thank your guest.**
   Say, "Thanks for coming in. Have a wonderful day!"

9. **Clean your station before your next guest.**

During the 2-Minute Plan you will want to follow the same listening and observing process that was suggested in the consultation phase of the service.

Remember that you connect with your guest from the beginning to the very end of each of your experiences together. You need to stay focused on what's best for your guest. Is it the best thing for her to use drugstore products or another product line other than the one you retail in your salon or school? Is it best for her to go to another salon or school for her next service? If you answer no to these final questions, then make sure to make the 2-Minute Plan your new service completion process.

Think of the 10 Opportunities and 2-Minute Plan as your scripts to performing your role as a knowledgeable image expert. You will learn new scripts throughout your career; it is important to memorize and rehearse them.

Connecting Tip   #19

2-Minute Plan

Use the 2-Minute Plan to complete every service. Focus your attention on helping your guest to maintain her image by suggesting products and follow-up services. Satisfied guests will refer their friends and family, so don't forget to give them your business cards.

The Service Experience Follow-up

What can you do to connect with your guests in between services? Two great ways include follow-up calls and thank-you notes.

The Follow-Up Call

Ensure your guest is enjoying her new look by giving her a follow-up call.

Your follow-up call script:

Ask *"Hi, (guest name). It's (your name) from (salon). Do you have a moment?"* If you have caught the guest at a bad time, offer to call back at a better time. Ask what time would be convenient.

Say *"I just wanted to follow up to make sure your hair (cut, color, perm) is working well for you."* Wait for your guest to describe how she is feeling about the service. It is extremely important that your client knows you are listening and interested.

Ask *"Are you able to style your hair the way you wanted?"* or *"How does your color or perm look after you style your hair?"* Again, let your guest answer. Respond to your guest in a calm and relaxed manner.

Ask You may also ask about her product purchase. *"How are you enjoying your products?"* or *"Do you have any questions about how to use them?"*

Thank your guest when you receive a positive response. You may also confirm the next appointment or make a suggestion to schedule another appointment.

Say *"I am happy that you are enjoying your products and hair (or other service results). We'll see you (date/time). (Or I hope to see you soon). Thank you for taking the time to speak with me."*

KATE

Kate Troc, founder of 20/20 FORESIGHT, has been an active member of the beauty industry for more than 20 years. She has played vital roles in the development, growth, and profitability of independent salons and national salon chains alike. Kate has excelled in key positions including hairdresser, salon manager, and vice president of operations for a national salon chain. Kate has fresh and creative ideas on how to build your business and connect with your guests.

Incredible success is yours for the taking. It, however, requires that you develop a newer and keener perspective of what your guests really want and what they define as "success." Creativity is extremely important. Finding ways to not just satisfy, but to surprise your guests by creating new and memorable experiences is where incredible success resides.

At first it may seem difficult to think about how to surprise your guests, but it absolutely applies to your business. Think differently about what you do. You are selling experiences and guiding your guests through transformations. When you increase the caliber of the experience you provide, you can increase your guest retention rates and your service prices. Why do you choose one restaurant over another — is it strictly the food? Not usually. More often it is the ambiance, attitude, and atmosphere — the overall experience.

Perhaps among the most difficult of life's challenges is how to make the old new again, and how to maintain or rekindle our passion for the things we do daily. Ironically, the better you become at the technical aspects of your profession, the more stagnant, complacent, and indifferent you may become in the process of delivering your service.

TROC

Make it your goal to perform in the salon or school instead of merely working in it. Keep your attitude and experience fresh, lively, and fun.

Find ways to surprise your guests:

- Welcome your guest with a special sign.
- Remember her birthday.
- Buy a bunch of single long-stemmed flowers and give one to each of your guests.
- Buy a lint brush and use it on her coat, then help her put it on.
- Give her a hand massage while her hair is processing.
- Create a fun environment that includes the guests.

> "Make it your goal to perform in the salon or school instead of merely working in it."

There are endless ways to create a unique experience and lasting impressions. Most ideas are minimal to no cost to implement. The emphasis is on approaching your work as a performance with the sales floor as your stage.

Once your stage is set to pleasantly surprise your guests, it's time to pay attention to your script. There is one true enemy in your drama: It is indifference. According to *US News* and *World Report*, 68 percent of customers who stopped buying from a particular company did so because of employee indifference toward their needs and wants; only 14 percent stopped buying because they were dissatisfied with the product. Your success is guaranteed when you consistently create memorable experiences that pleasantly surprise your guests.

Dealing With a Not-So-Positive Guest Response

If your client's response is not so positive, remember to listen and stay focused on solutions. View a guest's feedback as an opportunity to gain her loyalty by offering excellent follow-up service. The following are some suggestions for handling challenging responses:

- Ask questions about the challenge the guest is having.

- Listen patiently until you have resolved the challenge with your guest.

- Provide suggestions on how to correct the challenges. In extreme cases, offer to have your guest return so that you may look at her hair.

- Remain relaxed and calm. Your guest may not return if she thinks you are upset or angry.

- Say, *"I am happy we were able to create a follow-up plan, (guest's name). I just want you to know that I appreciate your business and want you to be completely satisfied with your looks and your products. I will see you on (date/time). Thank you."*

Send a Thank-You Note

Another great way to get your guest to fondly remember you is to send a thank-you note within two days of the service. Take a moment to thank your guest for her business and invite her back. You may want to enclose your business card with a reminder date and time of the scheduled appointment. See **Chapter 8** for more tips on writing thank-you cards.

If you really want to connect with your loyal guests, make a note of their birthdays and send birthday cards. This is a wonderful little surprise that will remind her of you and the unbelievable service and support you provide her.

Learn From Star Performers

 Successful beauty professionals who consistently provide unbelievable service attract and retain a large and prosperous clientele. Their goal is not to just offer good or satisfactory service, but to provide unbelievable client service. Star performers make great incomes by simply loving and caring for their guests. They know great service is good for business. So they continually develop their skills and direct their focus on their guests' wants and needs.

GAME PLAN

ACT
In this chapter you learned about developing a relationship to your clients. Let's create the third step of your game plan. Make a commitment to learn how to best service your client. **Write your commitment here.**

_____

REFLECT
Think about what fears or obstacles may interfere with keeping your commitment. **Write them here**.

_____

TAKE ACTION

PERFORM
Services are experiences. Create a lasting memory. Play the role of a knowledgeable image expert. Remember your guests are your audience.

CREATE
Use the 5 Senses Program to create a beautiful and comfortable service environment for your guests.

STAR
Review the Star Quality Checklist and make plans for how you will continually improve.

WELCOME
Use the Service Builders Checklist for answering the phone and welcoming guests.

CONNECT
Connect with your guest during the consultation to uncover what she likes and who she is. Agree upon a game plan. Stay connected throughout the entire service by using the 10 Opportunities.

COMPLETE
Make a service and product recommendation. Use the 2-Minute Plan to ensure your guest visits again.

"If you are in a room with your mentor, the one with the most experience should do the talking and the one with the least experience should be listening."

Andrew Gomez,
Von Curtis Academy graduate

LISTE

Chapter 6

My Mentors

Work smarter, not harder. In this chapter you will learn where to look for professional mentors and how to work with a mentor. A mentor is a teacher or leader who has the knowledge and experience to act as your guide. Mentors are one of the most valuable learning resources you have.

Learn to work smarter, not harder, by finding a mentor who has life experiences and perspectives that you do not. You don't personally have to go through all of life's lessons. That can be painful and time-consuming. But you can choose to learn from other people's successes and experiences.

Speed up your learning process by being coachable. That means you are open to learning and taking advice. All around you there are people who want you to succeed and are willing to help.

There is a wealth of knowledge and experience that you could never attain by yourself, even in an entire lifetime. Mentors are there, waiting for you to learn from them. We will also talk about how you too can become a mentor and give guidance to others.

Learn from the wisdom and experience of others

Think about:

- Why do I need mentors in my life?

- What can I learn?

- What kind of mentoring do I need right now?

- How do I work with my mentor?

- How can I mentor others?

Learn about:

- Mentors are everywhere.

- Choosing a mentor.

- Learning from a mentor.

- Giving back as a mentor.

Learn from:

- Robert Cromeans

- Sister Bonnie Steinlage

Mentors Are Everywhere

Think of a time when your life felt like one big maze. You blindly tried to feel your way through the endless, winding life paths. Sometimes you were not sure of the way to go. You were lost in the endless detours. You may have been frustrated with how long it took to find your way.

Mentors are guides on your journey through life."

Now imagine if you would have had a mentor to go through the maze with you. Someone who was there saying, "Try this way" or "Go that way." The mentor would show you that the maze was just part of the process of learning and that your experiences—no matter how challenging—can be fun.

Mentors are guides on your journey through life. They help you to clarify what is important. Without a mentor, you are left with a limited perception of yourself. Through a mentor's perspective, you can broaden your view and widen your options.

What is really great is that there are mentors all around you. They may be the person in the chair next to you, a client, a parent, or a famous person. Most successful people spend time with mentors.

Winn Claybaugh's Mentors

Winn Claybaugh is owner of MASTERS, a monthly audio program in which he interviews successful people in the beauty industry. He is also co-founder of PAUL MITCHELL THE SCHOOL. Winn has had many mentors over the years. He tells us about them here:

One of my greatest mentors was a recovering alcoholic. This man taught me incredible things about self-esteem and how to overcome personal challenges. Did I also need to become an alcoholic in order to learn the great lessons of life that my mentor learned? No. But I adopted him as a mentor so that I could bypass what he went through and still reap the benefits of his wisdom.

On John Paul DeJoria

John Paul DeJoria's philosophy and support have helped me in many areas of my life. Many times he has said to me, "Successful people do all of the things that unsuccessful people don't want to do." I have applied his philosophy to many areas of my life. For an example, if you go to the gym at 6 a.m., you will find the place is packed. Is it packed with the unhealthy, unmotivated people? No. Unsuccessful people are still in bed.

On Trevor Sorbie

When I interviewed Trevor Sorbie, he told me that after receiving the British Hairdresser of the Year award for the second time, he ended up in the hospital with severe depression and truly believed that he would never work again. Somehow he overcame his setback and went on to build an empire. He went on to receive the British Hairdresser of the Year award two more times. Trevor has inspired me to focus on learning how to be happy. If he can do it, I can do it, too.

On Jeanne Braa

Jeanne Braa, who is one of my long-time mentors and friends, is one of the most talented and popular stage artists. However, she had to overcome great obstacles in the beginning. She was so poor earlier in her career that she had to take a loan out on her sewing machine, to buy a plane ticket to see Paul Mitchell on stage. She retired a multimillionaire. She has taught me to seek out and surround myself with successful people.

On Joe Dudley

During his interview, Joe Dudley shared the fact that at the age of five, he was labeled "mentally retarded." It wasn't until years later, when his girlfriend told him that she wouldn't marry him because she didn't want to have stupid children, that he finally decided to get an education. He went on to earn a Ph.D. He is now one of the largest manufacturers of ethnic hair products in the world and has met with national leaders like South Africa's Nelson Mandela. Dr. Dudley has inspired me to become a lifelong learner.

Successful people do all of the things that unsuccessful people don't want to do."

On Van Council

Van Council, a very successful salon owner and platform artist, has had a speech impediment his entire life. In addition, he had a very strong Southern accent. In the beginning of his career, his clients couldn't understand what he was saying. He didn't allow this to hold him back, however. Since people often thought he was foreign, he decided to use their perception to his advantage. He figured that foreign hairdressers could charge extra money for their haircuts. He charges $150 and has three salons that do a total business of $14 million per year. He has motivated me to go for my goals.

Finding Mentors

A mentor does not necessarily need to be a famous person who owns a company or the author of a book. Think about the goals you have outlined in previous chapters. In **Chapter 1** and **Chapter 2** you outlined your learning and personal development goals. In **Chapter 3** you identified your image goals. **Chapter 4** developed your goals about your business and technical tools. **Chapter 5** outlined your client service goals. Now look for people who have successfully worked on each of these goals. They are your mentors.

For example, your goal is to develop your client service skills. Find a mentor who has a great clientele. Or you may want to learn how to be an instructor. Find a successful instructor who can guide you. Maybe you want to open your own salon. Work with a salon owner. Think of each goal and ask yourself how a mentor may help you to grow and who that mentor may be.

Where do you look for mentors? Go where successful people work and hang out. Successful people, your potential mentors, are continually focused on things that help them grow professionally and personally. You can find your mentors at work, at social events, at educational events, in publications, and in professional organizations. **Chapter 7** provides professional resources used to connect with potential mentors.

WHERE TO FIND MENTORS

① Shows and educational events

② Classes with guest artists or educators

③ Online communities

④ Audio tapes, video tapes, or books

⑤ Professional organizations and associations

⑥ Professional product company

⑦ Local salon to contact a local salon owner, educator, or company leader

Network and Search

Talk about your goals with people you know. Your friends, family, and co-workers may be able to help you find a mentor who is perfect for what you would like to learn.

Research the industry magazines listed in **Chapter 7**. They feature top industry artists and salons. Read the magazines regularly. The chances are that you will find a mentor for your goals.

Once you have identified a mentor, do a little research on this person. Most famous people have a bio or personal story. Send your potential mentor an introductory letter and request an in-person or phone interview. Your potential mentor will most likely be flattered and very interested in helping you. Remember, however, successful people are also very busy, so you may have to be patient in getting your interview. In preparation, create several questions that will help you to learn about the person.

Connecting Tip   #20

Find Mentors

There are people all around you who would love to help and support you.

• Work smarter, rather than harder. Find mentors you would love to connect with and learn from them.

• Spend time with people you are interested in, who are supportive of you and who accelerate your learning process.

ROBERT CROMEANS

Robert Cromeans, a native of Glasgow, Scotland, came to the US in 1985 and was soon discovered by the legendary Jeanne Braa. He quickly established himself as one of the brightest lights in the beauty industry. He is known for innovation and daring design. As creative director at John Paul Mitchell Systems, Robert educates hairdressers around the world. Robert has recorded two audio learning series called "The Art Of Making Money" and "BS: Belief System" in which he shares his industry experiences.

First, I want to ask you, "Why do you want to be a hairdresser?" Is it the lure of creative freedom? Or the way people look in the industry? What made the connection for you?

I was initially attracted because of the fashion. I was very intrigued by outstanding looking people who were really well-dressed. Their images told a great story. I wanted to connect with that kind of freedom of personal expression. Essentially, they were the first image mentors I wanted to emulate.

People often compare hairdressers to artists because artists have unusual perspectives on life. The only thing that I hate about being called an artist is the "starving artist" image. I think that's an old mentality. What we do can be art, but I think hairdressing is truly a business. For those of you who choose hairdressing for art and expressiveness—yahoo! You're going to have a lot of fun. But one of the greatest opportunities you have is the possibility to make money. Being creative while making money, now doesn't that sound fun?

Find people who inspire you in your business, as well as help you develop your creativity. Fifteen years ago, I went to a beauty school in Memphis, Tennessee.

I learned about this incredible renegade Scotsman named Paul Mitchell. I loved his products and approach to hairdressing right from the start. I began to believe in his company. I actually purchased products using my own money so that I could play the professional game right away while in beauty school.

In essence, my first business mentor was the Paul Mitchell Company. This may not sound like it's a mentorship, but in reality, I think companies may be your best business resources. A company can be more connected to the whole industry than one individual person.

> "Being creative while making money, now doesn't that sound fun?"

Jeanne Braa was one of the most incredible hairdressers in the world. She had the most magical hands. I had two left thumbs and never touched hair until I was 24 years old. So I had to hang around someone who could make hairdressing look like ballet. Jeanne was my greatest mentor.

There are hundreds of great professionals, people like Trevor Sorbie, Vidal Sassoon, Irvine Rusk, and Robert Lobetta. They all started doing hair as teenagers. When I started, Mr. Sassoon had been doing hair seven years already! Does that mean I could never be as great as he is? No. What I had to do is accelerate my learning. Staying focused and finding mentors can help you learn quickly.

Being Coachable

 It is amazing how much you can absorb just by being in the presence of a mentor. No amount of mentoring will help, however, if you aren't open to coaching.

Listen — The most important thing to remember is to listen to your mentor. If someone is willing to give you her time, experience, and life history, listen with respect and treat the information that you receive like gold. Be open-minded to a new approach and perspective. We talked about "emptying your cup" in **Chapter 2.** Remember sometimes you have to let go of what you think you know so that you can be open to new ideas.

Effort and focus — Next realize that learning from a mentor involves effort and focus. When given the opportunity to learn from masters, be present and focus on what they have to offer. Forget about the next break from class or what you are going to have for lunch, and focus on learning.

Seize the moment — Take full advantage of having a mentor in one of your classes by asking to assist them. Offer to pack up her tools, sweep up hair, or help with models. Stay after class to ask questions. You can make any class you attend into a mini-mentoring session by seizing the present moment as an opportunity to learn.

Show appreciation — Finally, treat your mentors with respect. Find ways to thank them. The best thanks of all is to take what she has given you and put it into action. Even the most patient mentors may become frustrated with you if you don't take their suggestions and make changes. Follow up with your mentor by sending thank-you notes or e-mails about your progress.

WORKING WITH YOUR MENTOR

1 Show up early and stay late.

2 Be present and focused on what you are learning.

3 Do whatever it takes to learn. Assist your mentors. Be willing to fold towels, clean, and help them in any way you can.

4 Pay attention to everything your mentor does. Mentors are masters at what they do. By paying attention to the smallest details, you may learn a valuable tip that can save you time or help you to make more money.

5 Look your professional best. Successful people look the part. If you want to hang out with your mentors show that you care about what they think. Look your best.

6 Take what your mentor gives you and find ways to implement it immediately. Review the learning practices in **Chapter 2**.

7 Realize that your mentors have special knowledge and information. Not everything they share may apply to you. Take what you can use and leave the rest.

In **Chapter 2**, we said that one of the best ways to learn is to teach. Although you may be just starting your career, there are many ways you can give back to your school, your community, and your profession. You can mentor others in a variety of ways.

Be a new professional mentor — Remember your first day of school or in the salon and how nervous you were? Imagine if you would have been assigned a mentor. Someone who showed you the ropes, calmed your nerves, and guided you. Become a mentor to new students or team members by helping them as they make the transition into a new routine and culture. Your support can be a tremendous help to new classmates and team members.

Giving Back – You as the Mentor

Be a potential professional mentor – There are lots of people interested in entering the beauty industry. You can help potential professionals by offering your support and perspective on what you have experienced. Be a goodwill ambassador for the industry by answering questions and sharing its benefits. We can't learn everything through firsthand experience because it takes too long and the sacrifice it would take to learn the lessons would be too great.

Be a volunteer – Be a beauty mentor. Find ways you can give your time to others who need your expertise about beauty and image. Help to build the self-esteem and confidence of someone in need. Contact local community organizations to learn how you can help others by offering your services to youth groups, shelters, or nursing homes.

Be a nice mentor – In **Chapter 1**, you learned it is important to be nice. Share what you've learned with others. Being a nice mentor could be one of the most important mentoring roles you may ever have.

Be a learning mentor – Share what you have learned in this book. Help others to connect to their future by passing on this information and other things you learn. Make it a goal to share new information with your clients, classmates, teammates, friends, and family. A successful mentor's time is very valuable. Make the most of your mentoring experience.

> *We can't learn everything through firsthand experience because it takes too long and the sacrifice it would take to learn the lessons would be too great."*

> *A successful mentor's time is very valuable. Make the most of your mentoring experience."*

Connecting Tip   #21
Be Coachable

- Be focused and prepared.
- Let go of what you think you know to make room for new ideas.
- Do whatever it takes to learn. Arrive early, stay late.
- Look your most professional.
- Find ways to implement what your mentor teaches you immediately.
- Open up to a new perspective without resistance.

SISTER BONNIE

In 1986, Sister Bonnie Steinlage, a member of the Franciscan Sisters of the Poor for 38 years, embarked on a new life mission. She began providing salon care to poor and often homeless people. Sister Bonnie's compassion has led to partnerships with major businesses and salon professionals who have helped her in her work.

One Ash Wednesday I heard a reading from the Gospel of Matthew: "When you fast and pray, wash your face and groom your hair." I translated this to mean that after Mass I should go for a new hairdo. I felt that if I was going to fast and pray for 40 days, I had better look up to the challenge.

While I was sitting in the chair at the beauty salon, I was inspired to become a hair stylist. I could serve the poor and homeless by offering hair services. This was the beginning of my journey. I knew this decision was going to change my life. There were, however, several things I had to do. First, I had to get permission from the leadership of the Franciscan Sisters of the Poor. This was a highly unusual request for a 43-year-old Sister. I wrote a letter and, to my delight, was granted permission.

After finishing school, I immediately began working at the Mary Magdalene House, providing hair services. A volunteering hairdresser, Vernon Ferrier, was an excellent support to our cause. One day he offered to take me to my first hair show. There I had the opportunity to meet a very generous person. That was Fred Holzberger, the owner of Fredric's Corporation, distributors of Aveda products.

We began talking and Fred was astonished to find out that I was a Sister. He was so intrigued that he invited me to a special luncheon. When I arrived, he asked if I could say a few words to the group, which numbered around 200 people. As I was talking, he became very emotional, but I wasn't sure why. I later learned that as a little boy his father had died, and the Franciscan Sisters provided clothing and food to his struggling family.

STEINLAGE

At the end of my talk, Mr. Holzberger came up on stage and pledged that he would supply all the products we needed for our services. The corporation later went far beyond its original commitment and converted a Winnebago trailer into a traveling salon. It travels a tri-state area, visiting a variety of community centers, and providing services to hundreds of people.

> "The touch you provide as a hairdresser or esthetician is very intimate and can be a powerful opportunity to help others."

I have come to realize that the beauty services offered by professionals are an exchange of healing energy that can build confidence and self-esteem. I see every salon as a place where people are rejuvenated and nurtured. The touch you provide as a hairdresser or esthetician is very intimate and can be a powerful opportunity to help others.

I once completed a haircut on a homeless gentleman who hadn't seen his face in years. He could not recognize himself with his new look. He didn't want to leave my chair. He was so cold and frozen, and my chair was the most comfort he had felt in a long time. Many people we care for at our salons have not been groomed, touched, or cared for in years.

When I cut a homeless person's hair, I try to create a totally new look. This can be a key to new opportunities. People no longer look frightening, and they have access to warm places in the winter and cool places in the summer. They may be able to apply for housing or a job. The things they were previously denied become opportunities, just by changing their looks. I believe that the services Salon Professionals provide can truly help others make a fresh start.

God Doesn't Play Favorites

There are a variety of mentors you can learn from to grow spiritually, creatively, technically, personally, and professionally. Mentors are everywhere; you just need to look for them and make them a part of your life. Allow them to help you to expand your thinking and experience. If you do not have mentors, you are left with a limited perception of yourself.

A wise person learns from other people's experiences rather than learning everything firsthand. A mentor shows you the way. Mentors help you learn amazing lessons through their experiences. God does not play favorites. God does not give one person more potential than someone else. A mentor can help you to see that.

Have you ever been to a museum and stood in front of a piece of art that gave you goose bumps, or even brought tears to your eyes? The reason great art or great music thrills you is because it wakes up something deep inside that reminds you that you have the same potential to create brilliance. The only difference between you and the masters is time. If they did it, you can, too. You're just a couple of steps behind them. So, have fun and learn with a mentor, but more importantly, learn how to be a mentor.

> *Have fun and learn with a mentor, but more importantly, learn how to be a mentor."*

Connecting Tip   #22

Give Back

You don't need 30 years of experience to mentor and give back to others. You can lend a hand to a new student or teammate, provide encouragement to potential students, or give back to a client in need. You have the power to make a difference in people's lives.

MY MENTORS
GAME PLAN

LISTEN
In this chapter you learned about finding mentors for your professional career. Let's create the sixth step of your game plan. Make a commitment to finding your mentors. **Write your commitment here.**

_____

REFLECT
Think about what fears or obstacles may interfere with keeping your commitment. **Write them here.**

_____

TAKE ACTION

FIND
Work smarter, not harder, by learning from other people's experiences. Find mentors for every part of your life.

LEARN
Identify what you would like to learn, whom you can learn from, and how you can contact them.

OPEN
Listen with an open mind. Do whatever it takes to learn.

FOCUS
Make your next class a mini-mentoring session, by volunteering your help. Show up early and stay late. Be focused on what is being taught and how it is presented.

THANK
Appreciate your mentors. Say thank you by following their advice.

GIVE
Give back by mentoring new and Future Professionals.

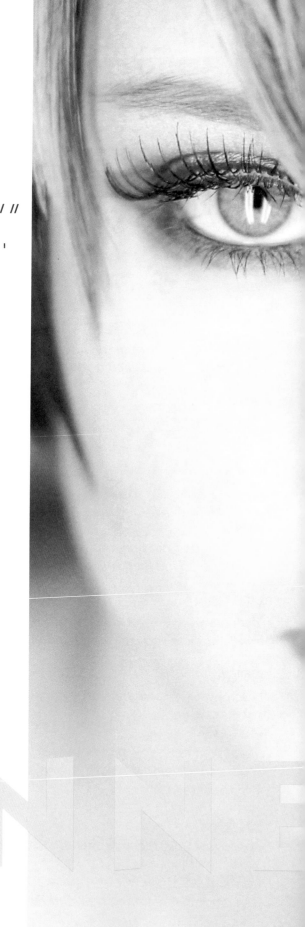

"Just say 'yes'."

Winn Claybaugh

CON NE

Chapter 7

My Future

Say "yes" to your future. There are opportunities everywhere within this great industry. It is important for you to say "yes" to all of the experiences that are presented to you. There are shows, education, and industry events to attend. Just say "yes!"

There are valuable school functions and activities that you may take advantage of. Just say "yes!" You have opportunities to participate in salon events, ongoing training, and team meetings. Just say "yes" to learning and growing with your team.

New opportunities will not materialize right in front of your eyes. You have to search for them. This chapter is a guide to what you may experience and achieve. Start taking advantage of the opportunities within the industry by becoming active while in school and staying active throughout your career. Join the thousands of others who connect and learn through events, educational classes, online communities, and professional associations.

Connecting with other professionals and industry organizations will bring you new opportunities to learn. Your participation and efforts will be rewarded with new clients, career opportunities, professional satisfaction, and personal wisdom. Connect and achieve beyond what you believe is possible.

CT

Connect with your future

Think about:

- What is happening in the beauty industry?

- How will I get involved with the industry?

- What resources could I use to learn more about my profession?

- How can I expand my career experience?

- How can I support my salon by participating in salon events, community events, and other activities?

Learn about:

- Just say "yes" to connecting.
- School activities.
- Salon events.
- Your profession.

Learn from:

- The International Haircolor Exchange
- North American Hairstyling Awards
- Behind The Chair
- The Salon Association

Just Say "Yes" to Connecting

The beauty industry is so much more than the four walls of your school or salon. Although you will find wonderful inspiration from your clients, your team members, and team leaders, you need to expand your vision beyond your daily experiences.

It's important to avoid falling into the daily rut of getting up, going to work or school, serving clients, and coming home. You will quickly get bored. If you are currently feeling uninspired, start exploring. Open your mind and say "yes" to getting connected. If you are not currently connected to the industry, don't wait. You deserve to have fun, pursue new interests, and "play" in one of the most entertaining industries in the world. All you have to do is say "yes" to exploring the possibilities.

Say "Yes" to Joining

 One of the benefits of being part of the beauty industry is meeting the people who are part of it. The industry is filled with talented, creative, and interesting professionals who are unlike any other professional group. They are known for their creativity, their commitment to social issues, and their love of learning. As a member of this exciting industry you must network with others. The more connected you are, the easier it will be to build your business and professional reputation. To learn and benefit from others in the industry, all you have to do is say "yes" to joining and learning.

The beauty industry offers many fun learning activities including shows, events, seminars, networking groups, and school and salon activities. All you have to do is show up and be open to learning from these experiences. The ideas in this chapter are not things you must do. They are things you have the opportunity to do!

Connect with School Activities

Start to connect while you are in school. There are opportunities to learn everywhere. You are investing time, money, and resources, so make sure that you get a return on your investment instead of just going through the motions. Push yourself to learn something every chance you get. Start by joining in extracurricular activities. They allow you to connect with people you may otherwise never have the opportunity to interact with.

Student Programs

The following are examples of student programs offered at PAUL MITCHELL THE SCHOOL. The programs are referred to as "student run" programs, meaning that they are operated by students. Future Professionals who make a commitment by being involved are more likely to get the most out of their education. The student programs are fun learning opportunities that provide access to a variety of mentors, including instructors, salon owners, hairdressers, and industry artists.

Each program has a different focus. As you read the program descriptions, you may consider joining or starting a similar program in your school.

student rep
PROGRAM

The Student Rep Program – Retail sales and management is a major focus of business within the professional beauty industry. The Product Rep program focuses on the basic skills needed to develop and maintain a successful retail center within a salon or spa. It includes everything you need to know to operate a successful product retail center from promotion planning to basic accounting procedures.

Members of the Product Rep team apply for positions and actually interview with an advising school team leader. The team works together to maintain the school product retail store area. The experience is extremely beneficial for those aspiring to become top retail salespeople, retail store managers, salon managers, or product account executives.

Student Council — The Student Council is a student-run advisory board and special events team. The council consists of six to 10 members chosen by the student body for their willingness to participate and contribute to the team's success. The group contributes to the entire student body's learning experience by sponsoring activities that are positive, fun, and uplifting. The council works to establish better communication and harmony within the school. It sponsors team-building events such as welcome pancake breakfasts for new students and birthday celebrations. They organize special recognitions like Future Professional of the Month, Learning Leader of the Month, special contribution awards, and mentor awards.

Get involved or help to organize a Student Council at your school. It is a great way to learn how to work within a team. Such experience is extremely beneficial if you plan to work in a large salon or corporate organization.

Design Team — The Design Team is a community relations team that assists in promoting the school within local high schools and the community. The team attracts potential students and new clients to the school through outreach activities, including high school events, college fairs, fashion shows, beauty pageants, and local TV and film announcements. Team members develop creative hairdressing techniques and professional presentation skills. The Design Team activities develop your presentation and public relations skills.

Organize a special interest group or club. Get together, have fun, and create."

Special Interest Clubs

There are a variety of special interest clubs that may be organized. These clubs bring together students with similar interests or aspirations. Clubs provide the opportunity to network and receive specialized training to enhance and accelerate certain skills. Organize a special interest group or club. Get together, have fun, and create. Here are a few examples:

Long Hair or Classical Hairdressing Club — This club focuses on the art of classical hairdressing including updos, hair extensions, and hairpieces. Club members master specific looks, organize photo shoots, or prepare for hairdressing competitions. They invite skilled professionals to share their skills or watch technical videos on such masters as Jeanne Braa, Suzanne Chadwick, Vivienne Mackinder, or Martin Parsons. Club members gain classical hairdressing skills used to service clients attending weddings, proms, and other special events.

Color Club — This club focuses on mastering the art of hair coloring. Successful industry colorists invest time and education dollars in learning these creative techniques. A Color Club can be an inexpensive, practical learning opportunity that could feature a mentor colorist, showcasing creative techniques or technical hair color videos. The Color Club invites talented local colorists to work with the group to provide inspiration and education on a variety of technical skills.

Makeup Club — This club focuses on mastering the art of makeup. Members develop knowledge of color theory, makeup products, techniques, and applications. The team invites guest makeup artists to demonstrate techniques. Work on developing your photography skills and corrective and creative makeup techniques. Assist with school photos shoots and theatrical productions.

Men's Style Club — This club focuses on building a business in one of the fastest growing segments of the beauty industry: the men's market. Club members learn unique approaches to building a male clientele and the technical skill development to mastering men's cutting, sideburns, and hair styling.

Theatrical Club — This club focuses on hair and makeup for the stage or film. The club members connect with local theaters to observe or support backstage preparation during a production. It can be the driving force behind producing successful student shows.

These are just a few examples of how you could take your special interests and make them into a group learning and networking experience. If your school doesn't currently have clubs like these, ask permission to start one.

THE INTERNATIONAL HAIRCOLOR EXCHANGE

The International Haircolor Exchange, IHE, is a nonprofit organization for the professional hair colorist. Its goal is to create an atmosphere of pure education and sharing where everyone and all facets of the industry are equal. A place where manufacturers and professionals alike can be both teacher and student—all together, learning, and sharing.

The organization was founded and is run by a board of hair colorists who volunteer throughout the year to host The Exchange, the very best arena where hair colorists share techniques and formulas.

The International Haircolor Exchange mission includes:

* To promote and elevate the image of the professional hair color specialist.

* To increase the knowledge and skills of the membership of the International Haircolor Exchange, which will aid in placing them at the top of their profession.

* To aid in establishing standardized methods for teaching hair coloring, which would promote a greater number of hair color specialists in the field and set an example to young hair colorists entering our profession.

* To create a professional networking system that encourages a free exchange of ideas and information among the membership.

* To make available to our educational institutions any hair color information that will aid in producing a more competent graduate.

* To interface with hair color manufacturers in product and technical development.

The board selects a group of artists from every facet of the salon industry. Each guest artist and manufacturer shares his or her ideas and innovations in an on-stage segment.

The International Haircolor Exchange is always looking for ways to increase awareness and offer education to the colorist.

**For more information visit us
on the Web at www.int-haircolor-ex.org
or call 1-800-COLOR55.**

Additional School Events

Here are some other examples of how you may learn to connect with your school, future employers, and the industry.

Student Shows — Many schools host annual or biannual student shows providing students the opportunity to work within a group to produce and showcase their work. Everyone on the team can benefit from this experience, whether you are in charge of ticket sales, promotion, model recruitment, model prep, choreography, wardrobe, or show production. Students advertise at local nightclubs, high schools, women's clubs, and salons.

Competitions/Contests — Many salon organizations and trade shows sponsor technical competitions. Hundreds of Future Professionals and new professionals compete in hair styling, haircutting, men's cutting, updo and fantasy hair styling, and hair coloring competitions. Schools like PAUL MITCHELL THE SCHOOL in Provo, Utah, hold annual team sales contests, like "The Caper." Groups of Future Professionals compete to meet predetermined retail sales goals. Successful teams earn their way to the ISSE trade show in California.

Career/Job Fairs — Some schools offer events to network with potential employers, like career or job fairs. The school invites the top salons in the region or country to speak directly with Future Professionals. During school-sponsored career fairs, salon owners share their company's opportunities and explain the interview process and hiring criteria. Career fairs are opportunities to clarify what you would like in a future employer and work environment.

Photo Shoots — School photo shoots help you to develop a portfolio of your work and to collect photos to submit to magazines or photo work competitions, like the one sponsored by North American Hairstyling Awards (NAHA). Future Professionals from various clubs or from the general student body participate by doing a model's hair and makeup. The school can arrange to find an up-and-coming student photographer who may also need to develop his or her portfolio. The school team helps to organize the event, and participants pay a fee to cover expenses.

See **Chapter 4** for details on how to create a portfolio and organize a photo shoot.

NORTH AMERICAN HAIRSTYLING AWARDS

The North American Hairstyling Awards is an editorial photo competition that is held every year. It is the Oscars of the beauty industry. NAHA celebrates the artistry of stylists in nine different technical categories. Winners receive recognition from the press and from the industry.

You will benefit from entering the photo competition in the student category whether you win or not. Your participation provides the experience of doing quality editorial work early in your career while most students are focusing on passing their state boards.

Start planning your entry now. Learn everything from balancing all the aspects of a photo shoot and working with the photographer, to completing the makeup and hair and coordinating the fashion. Putting it all together and submitting your work will be very satisfying and a great learning experience.

We will be happy to answer all of your questions about the competition and send you a copy of *The Inside Track to NAHA*, written by 1991 North American Hairstylist of the Year Mary Brunetti. The book provides great tips for entering and gaining the edge on competition.

North American Hairstyling Awards (NAHA)
15825 North 71st Street, Suite 100
Scottsdale, AZ 85254

TOLL FREE	1-800-468-2274
LOCAL	1-480-281-0424
FAX	1-480-905-0708
E-MAIL	naha@bbsi.org
WEB	www.one roof.org/naha

Connect With Your Salon

If you are leaving school and entering a salon, you need to be aware of your new role as a team member within your new professional home. Although being new on the team seems a little intimidating, it is important for you to get involved and support all salon activities right away.

Just Say "Yes" to Your Salon

 Your salon owner and manager will be impressed with your openness to try new things and support the salon. But be aware that "yes" has a bad rap. You may notice that some people in the salon look down on enthusiastic new people. They may even be critical of people who are willing to go the extra mile, calling you a "yes person." Unfortunately, they miss all of the opportunities that saying "yes" provides. The "habit of yes" is about being interested in what you are doing and who you are doing it with. Examples of salon experiences that you will want to enthusiastically support include:

Salon Meetings — Staff meetings are not for complaining and finding fault. They are for celebrating, brainstorming, creating solutions, and building relationships. Be willing to contribute and collaborate with your team to create a fun and productive work environment. Enter every team meeting with the question, "What's in it for us?"

Connecting Tip   #23

Just Say "Yes"

Just say "yes" to all opportunities available to you.

- Attend educational events.
- Compete in creative competitions.
- Create a special interest group.
- Do a photo shoot.

Salon Education — Most successful salons have training programs. Make sure to attend every class and seminar. Education is an investment that your leaders are making in you as a professional. So don't just show up; make sure to attend open to learn something new. It is unattractive to be a know-it-all and not support team education.

Salon Service/Product Launches — One of the most important and interesting things you can talk to your clients about is what is new. Clients love to be updated on the trends. Many salons feature various products and service promotions that will help you to service your client more effectively, but will also help you and your team be financially successful.

Photo Shoots — As outlined earlier in the school segment, photo shoots are a great way to document your artistic growth and gain recognition. Work with your salon to sponsor photo shoots. Put the photos on the walls of the salon or into a portfolio. See **Chapter 4** for ideas on how to prepare for a photo shoot.

Manufacturer/Product Distributor Shows — All salons have relationships with distributors and manufacturers. These companies host a variety of shows that you can attend or even assist with backstage preparation.

> *Education is an investment that your leaders are making in you as a professional."*

Connecting Tip   #24

Just Say "Yes" to your Salon

There are so many ways to get involved in the industry with your salon team. Don't allow other people's negativity to get you down. Say "yes" to participating in salon meetings, salon education, salon service promotions, and product launches. Help your salon to connect with the community. Organize and support events such as fundraisers, fashion shows, consumer events, or just simply have fun with a special salon day. Give back to your team and your community.

Salon Events

In-salon client events are a great way to attract new business and build client loyalty. Here are some examples of salon events you may have the opportunity to learn from:

- **Community events** — Community events include neighborhood or business association parties, sidewalk sale days, or Chamber of Commerce-sponsored events.

- **In-salon consumer education events** — Some salons love to help educate their clients by providing in-salon education events focusing on beauty tips including makeup, hair styling, skin care, body care, and nail care.

- **Fundraisers** — Help raise funds for charities, ecological organizations, or community programs. Clients generously support and choose companies and professionals who are socially conscious and giving.

- **Fashion shows** — Develop a salon fashion show for your clients and the local community. Give the proceeds to a local charity while spreading the word about beauty and fashion.

- **Special Salon Days** — Some salons sponsor special days that may include holiday themes, vacation themes, or quirky, fun themes.

  One salon created "Prom Day." Team members dressed in their high school prom dresses, posted their prom pictures, and had fun swapping stories with their clients.

Connect With the Professional Beauty Industry

There are many paths for you to follow that will help you to connect with your new profession. Each path can be fulfilling and inspiring, but all paths are not for everyone. After some exploration you will find your niche, then just stay involved. The following is a list of ways you may connect with professional beauty and salon businesses.

Shows — There are a variety of shows that are produced by various groups, organizations, and companies. All you need to do to get inspired is to show up. There are many different types of shows.

- **Manufacturer/product distributor shows** —
  The industry is filled with companies that create professional and retail products for the salon and spa industry. Product manufacturers commonly use the artistic approach to marketing new products and technical trends. A manufacturer's shows provide you with that company's interpretation of trends.
  Call your local product distributors for show dates.

- **Trade shows** — Trade shows are usually sponsored by industry organizations or trade show companies and are held at conference centers. They feature a variety of equipment, products, and educational companies all eager to sell their product supplies and tools.
  Trade shows are scheduled all over the world and throughout the year. Some of the largest include International Salon and Spa Expo (ISSE), Midwest Beauty Show, and International Beauty Show (IBS).

Specialty Shows — If you have a special interest in hair color or esthetics, you may want to check out shows that focus on hair color, makeup, esthetics, or nails. These include Hair Color USA, International Haircolor Exchange, International Esthetics, Cosmetic and Spa Conference, International Congress of Esthetics, The Nail Showcase, Western State Nail Expo, Nail Talk USA, and Nail Focus.

ATTENDING A TRADE SHOW

Shows are a wonderful way to network, learn about new trends, and connect with your professional community. Here are some important tips for attending any shows and educational events:

1 Dress up! Look fashionable and professional.

2 Be prepared. Bring a pen, paper, nametag, and business cards. Bring a full tool kit if you plan to attend a technical class.

3 Leave your cell phone at home. Stay focused on the show.

4 Arrive at all meetings, workshops, and gatherings at least 15 minutes early.

5 Sit in the front row.

6 Attend all scheduled events. Do not skip anything!

7 Stay to the end of the class. The best is often left to last, and most classes feature a grand finale.

8 Come with an open mind and heart. Do not critique the educators, the music, food, other attendees, the hotel, or entertainment. There is something to learn from everyone.

9 Remember that all eyes are on you. Be positive. If you don't feel positive, fake it.

10 When staying overnight, set an early curfew for yourself. Stay sober and be in your own bed no later than midnight.

11 When sharing a hotel room with a co-worker or fellow student, be respectful and do not invite friends into the room.

12 Respect others and their personal property.

13 Say "no" to unprofessional behavior. Remember that you are representing your school or salon. Make sure the impression you leave is a positive one. Have fun!

Note: These tips are based on an agreement that Future Professionals sign at PAUL MITCHELL THE SCHOOL when attending any industry event.

Connecting Tip   #25

Connect With Your Professional Community

Invest in yourself by:

- Attending shows and classes.
- Reading books and listening to audio tapes.
- Joining an association or organization.
- Visiting online resources.

Connect to Educational Resources

 One of the most exciting things about the beauty industry is that it is always changing and growing. Your future career path has many roads and opportunities to grow. Discover the ways you like to learn and continually focus on them. Make it a goal to learn something new each month. All of the following resources will expand your knowledge and vision.

Classes — Take time to learn from the masters in haircutting, hairdressing, makeup, skin care, and body care. Here are a few examples of great schools and academies: PAUL MITCHELL ADVANCED ACADEMY, ColorCutting USA, Toni & Guy Academy, Sebastian International Advanced Academy, Aveda Institutes, Vidal Sassoon Academy, Conservatory of Esthetics, International Dermal Institute, Pevonia International, Pivot Point International, and Gene Juarez Advanced Training Center.

Industry books/audio learning — There are wonderful learning tools within our industry, including books, audio tapes, and videos. Make it a habit to listen to audio tapes while you are exercising or driving. Read for 15 minutes every day or watch an educational video weekly. Your learning can be easily integrated into your daily lifestyle. For great educational resources go to *www.behindthechair.com* and *www.milady.com*.

Trade magazines/newsletters — There are many magazines that feature industry news and trends: *Modern Salon, Salon News, Salon Today, American Salon, American Spa, Dayspa, Salon Business Strategies* (newsletter)*, Canadian Hairdresser, Nail Pro,* and *Nail Magazine.*

Online communities — Check the Internet to learn more about educational facilities, manufacturers, and industry events. Hit these Web sites:

- *www.behindthechair.com*
- *www.salons.org*
- *www.paulmitchelltheschool.com*
- *www.salonemployment.com*

BEHIND THE CHAIR

Behindthechair.com, BTC, is a wonderful Internet resource dedicated to providing up-to-the-minute information and education.

It's graduation day. You get your license, say goodbye to all your girlfriends at school, and head off into the world of hairdressing. But, wait a minute. You have to find a job! You need to stay current with all the hottest hair and fashion trends, and you need to "keep the faith" when one of your haircuts doesn't turn out the way you hoped.

"**B**TC is the professional salon industry all together in one place with over 2,000 pages of cool stuff to read."

My name is Mary Rector-Gable, and I'm the founder of *behindthechair.com.* We're the largest online site in the world for Salon Professionals just like you. Our subscribers—over 55,000 of them—learn together, laugh together, cry together, and get inspired together. It's the professional salon industry all together in one place with over 2,000 pages of cool stuff to read. It's a place where you can find your first salon job at the best salon in town, hang out on the "Talkback" boards with other hairdressers, watch online technical videos from your favorite academies, or find out about all the latest cuts, trends, and products. And—drum roll, please—more than 200,000 hairdressers log on every month from around the world.

So, wanna hang with us? Log on to *behindthechair.com* and register to become a member. It's totally free. Once you're part of the family we send you weekly e-mails to keep you "in the know" on everything going on in the biz. This way you can enlighten all your friends and clients at the salon about the latest cuts and trends. And, if you're really nice, you'll even tell them how to get hooked up, too.

We'll see you online at *behindthechair.com.*
"MAN WE CAN—TOGETHER."
Mary Rector-Gable

CONNECT TO A PROFESSIONAL
ORGANIZATION

The following is a list of professional organizations that provide education and support.

Aestheticians International Association, Inc.
Sunnyvale, Texas
1-800-961-3777

Allied Beauty Association (ABA)
Ontario, Canada
(905) 568-0158
abacan@idirect.com

American Association of Cosmetology Schools (AACS)
Cosmetology Educators of America (CEA)
1-800-831-1086
www.beautyschools.org

American Beauty Association (ABA)
Chicago, Illinois
(312) 245-1595
www.abbies.org

American Board of Certified Master Hair Colorists (ABCMH)
San Pedro, California
(310) 547-0814

American Health and Beauty Aids Institute (AHBAI)
Chicago, Illinois
(312) 644-6610
ahbai@sba.com

American Massage Therapy Association (AMTA)
Evanston, Illinois
(847) 864-0123
info@inet.amtamassage.org

Associated Bodywork and Massage Professionals (ABMP)
Evergreen, Colorado
1-800-458-2267
expectmore@abmp.com

Beauty and Barber Supply Institute (BBSI)
Scottsdale, Arizona
1-800-211-4872
Erica@bbsi.org

Chicago Cosmetologist Association (CCA)
Chicago, Illinois
(312) 321-6809
isnow.com

Cosmetology Advancement Foundation (CAF)
New York, New York
For grant information:
(888) 411-GRANT

Intercoiffure (ICD)
New Orleans, Louisiana
(504) 288-9003
johnjay@gs.net

International Braiders Network
Brooklyn, New York
(718) 857-3811
tendrils@worldnet.att.net

International Nail Technicians Association (ICSA)
(312) 321-5161
isnow.com

International Guild of Professional Electrologists Inc. (IGPE)
High Point, North Caroline
1-800-830-3247
igpe@northstate.net

International Haircolor Exchange (IHE)
Memphis, Tennessee
1-800-COLOR-55
www.int-haircolor-ex.org

National Cosmetology Association (NCA)
Chicago, Illinois
1-800-527-1683

The Salon Association (TSA)
Scottsdale, Arizona
1-800-211-4872
www.oneroof.org

World International Nail and Beauty Association (WINBA)
Anaheim, California
(714) 779-9883

Dear Salon Professional:

The Salon Association is a professional organization dedicated to assisting salon owners and their teams. It sponsors educational events and an annual symposium and provides business resource information. Its mission is to provide opportunities for salon owners to share business solutions.

Membership:	**2,400 salon owners and leaders**
Founded:	**1996**
Member Benefits:	**Business benefits, services, and education designed to increase salon profitability, productivity, and success.**
National Education:	**Annual Business Symposium in January each year.**
Regional Education:	**Learning Lounges featured in five to six cities throughout the year.**

I often look at the salon industry with awe and inspiration. The chance to transform and uplift a human being is something extraordinary. When young people enter cosmetology school, they embark on a journey that is both professional and personal.

This journey will enhance your life by causing you to rethink all that you know. You will view people differently after your first client visit. You will appreciate co-workers more after your first client frustration. You will be more sympathetic after your client develops cancer and loses her hair. You will endure and learn to appreciate life in a very different way.

Sincerely,

Jill Kohler
TSA, Managing Director

If you are interested in joining, please call 1-800-211-4872
or write 15825 North 71st Street, Suite 100, Scottsdale, AZ 85254.
Visit us online at www.oneroof.org

MY FUTURE
GAME PLAN

CONNECT
In this chapter you learned about connecting to your future success. Let's create the seventh step of your game plan. Make a commitment to learning, joining, and saying "yes." **Write your commitment here.**

_____

REFLECT
Think about what fears or obstacles may interfere with keeping your commitment. **Write them here.**

_____

TAKE ACTION

EXPLORE
Say "yes" to exploring. You deserve to have fun, pursue new interests, and "play" in one of the most entertaining industries in the world. Just say "yes" to exploring possibilities.

BUILD
Say "yes" to joining. The more connected you are, the easier it will be to build your business and professional reputation.

SHOW UP
Say "yes" to learning. The beauty industry is full of many fun learning activities, including shows, events, seminars, networking groups, school activities, and salon activities.

SUPPORT
Support your team in all activities. Get your name out in the community by supporting your salon at its next event.

LEARN
Listen to audio tapes, watch videos, and read industry-focused books, magazines, and newsletters.

JOIN
Join a professional organization. Visit beauty-related Web sites and online communities.

"Ah, but a man's
reach should
exceed his grasp
or what's
a heaven for?"

Robert Browning,
English poet

PLAN

Chapter 8

My Plan

Growth. It's a fact of professional life. Do you have a clear vision of what you want to be, experience, and achieve? Or do you need help recognizing the greatness within you and the opportunities all around you?

The beauty industry is unique because it rarely experiences an economic downturn. Even in the toughest economic conditions, people want to look and feel better, and in the best of times people need a place to relax and rejuvenate. So, if you are good at what you do, you will grow.

In the days of the "beautician," a career in the industry was considered a "nontraditional" career choice. Beauty professionals were the people who couldn't afford or make it into college. Today that has all changed.

A career in the industry is now considered exciting, worthwhile, and cool. People in the know consider a career in the beauty and salon profession a legitimate lifestyle and career choice. Why? Because our industry is becoming increasingly more professional, innovative, and information-based. Salons, spas, and educational facilities are more sophisticated and service-savvy than in the past.

Now ask yourself, *What is my passion? What do I want to be when I grow up? What path do I want to take?* Hopefully the answers will become clearer as you read this chapter.

Create a road map for your journey

Think about:

- What do I want to do with my career?

- What holds me back?

- What tools do I need to promote myself?

- What steps should I take to get what I want?

- What do I want to become?

Learn about:

- Getting clear.

- Letting go.

- Creating a road map.

- Making it happen.

- Following your heart.

Learn from:

- Josh Banks

- Susie Fields

- Michael Cole

Your Journey Map

Although you may be near the end of this book, your journey is just beginning. With clarity, goals, and planning, you can get the career of your dreams. You will learn how to proceed on your journey to success. To simplify the process, we divided the journey into five steps to help you to work systematically toward your goals. The steps include:

Step 1 - Getting Clear	*What do I want to do with my career?*
Step 2 - Letting Go	*What holds me back?*
Step 3 - Creating a Road Map	*What tools do I need to promote myself?*
Step 4 - Making It Happen	*What steps do I take to get what I want?*
Step 5 - Following Your Heart	*What do I want to become?*

Step 1 Getting Clear

As your journey begins within the beauty industry, there are some specific things you can do to make sure that you create a path that is compatible with your interests, goals, and talents.

Start by thinking about what you want from the beauty and salon industry. For example, there are many Salon Professionals who simply want a job as a way to make a living. Do you want a job that will provide a comfortable living while you focus on other parts of your life? If so, that's cool. Positions within the salon industry can provide you with flexible work schedules that may fit your lifestyle.

Other professionals have found their life's calling within the industry. They have discovered their purpose and have integrated what they do to make money into their lifestyles. Their careers are how they live rather than how they make a living. If you want to build a career that is part of your lifestyle, you have also come to the right profession.

Both approaches to the profession are valid, but they provide different experiences and results. The word "career" is most frequently used to describe a person's life work, while a job is how you make money. It's important to clarify what you want from your profession. You can simply dabble in a job and make some cash, or you can create a deeply satisfying career that will ensure your ongoing prosperity, personal satisfaction, and growth. It's your choice.

Identify Your Interests and Talents

You may say, "I really don't know what I want to do!" The best way to get clear on what you want is to pay attention to what you love to do. For example, you may like to organize parties, you may love to help others, or you may love leading activities. Make a list of what energizes you and what you are good at.

I like to:

- Organize things.
- Have lots of friends.
- Learn.

_____

_____

_____

_____

_____

_____

_____

_____

I am good at:

- Details and follow-through.
- Socializing, networking, making friends.
- Helping and teaching others.

_____

_____

_____

_____

_____

_____

_____

_____

JOSH

Josh Banks began his hairdressing career in Scotland and eventually relocated to Toronto, Canada, where he managed one of the most creative and prestigious salons. There he began his platform artist career for Wella and became national artistic manager. Josh now co-owns the Kenneth George Salon and Spa in Los Angeles and is a nationally and internationally recognized guest artist for Wella USA. His work has been published in many magazines to include Modern Salon, Haircolor & Design, and Juice.

I have discovered during my career that the people who were most successful knew what they wanted and figured out how to get it. I would like to share with you five points that I think will help you to have fun on your career journey.

Start by thinking big. Do not limit yourself. You can go anywhere in the world and take your talents with you. Have a plan for getting what you want, but also be flexible and adjust your plan to accommodate the twists and turns in the road. You can experience multiple aspects of the industry during your career. You can be a great stylist, a successful educator, or a film and television stylist. Identify and reach for your destination by knowing where you want to go. When you know where you are going, you can get there faster and have more fun.

Ask, "What are my side streets?" Having a plan to get to your main destination is very important, but you also want to be able to adjust your route if necessary. An opportunity may come up, and you will take a side street. Sometimes the side streets are where you will have the most fun. When I was managing a salon in Canada, I was approached to get involved in shows and education. I thought, "I really want to go for that." From my success in shows, I was able to get involved in television and film work in Toronto. I enjoyed the media work so much that I set goals to get more work. My side-street opportunity helped me to clarify my goals.

BANKS

"*Continually look inside and be totally honest with yourself. Ask, What am I capable of? What talents do I have?*"

Surround yourself with people who can help you refuel. Look for people who will help you to stay inspired and motivated. Years ago I would watch Sonia and Christopher Dove, accomplished and well-known platform artists, on stage. I wanted to be like them.

Fifteen years later, I began working with them, and now they are among my best friends. They help me by sharing ideas and their passion for the industry. Look closely at the people who are in your life. If they are robbing you of energy or not supporting you, then replace them with friends, mentors, and peers who will support you.

Be OK with plan B. There is a possibility that you may not get exactly where you wanted to go. Ask yourself, *How would I feel if it takes me longer than I thought? How would I feel if I didn't get there at all?* This is important. Don't focus on what you are not achieving. If you make mistakes or take side steps, realize they are just steps to learning. Think of your mistakes as your learning opportunities.

Believe in yourself. Continually look inside and be totally honest with yourself. Ask, *What am I capable of? What talents do I have? What education do I have? What support do I have?* and *What do I want to go for?* Be grateful and confident because of what you have accomplished. Don't sell yourself short. But also don't forget to keep on learning.

Remember to believe in yourself. And if you ever see me at a show or a seminar, come up and talk to me. I would love to talk with you and share. Believe me, I will learn from you as much as you think you will learn from me.

Step 2 Letting Go

One of the biggest things that may hold you back from pursuing your dreams is fear. That little voice inside that says, "I could never do that! I won't make any money. What if I fail?" Clear your mind of messages that may hold you back. Let go of all the excuses that keep you from growing. Your fears are the roadblocks that will detour your journey.

When you are paying attention to what you want rather than what you don't want, you will discover that opportunities are everywhere just waiting for you to take action. Have you ever decided that you wanted something like a red Mustang convertible? Suddenly you see red Mustangs everywhere on the street, on television, and in magazines. Those red cars were always there, right? You just didn't notice them until you made the decision that you wanted one. Remember to focus on what you want. It will help you keep your mind clear.

Your Affirmation

Let's return to the beginning. In **Chapter 1**, we asked you to create an affirmation or confidence statement. Do you remember what your statement was? Let's create a new confidence statement or affirmation that addresses how you are feeling and thinking now. Here are some examples:

"I am successful."
"I know what I want."
"I am talented."
"I have the ability to make a lot of money."

Remember that your affirmations should be personal, in the present tense, and positive.

Replace self-limiting thoughts with life-affirming ones. Replace language that holds you back with language that helps you grow. Write your statements down and put them where you will see them often, like on your closet door or your mirror. Consistently focus on what you want to achieve. Dream big and ask yourself, "What could my career look like?" As you focus on your future vision, let go of the thoughts that hold you back.

> *Your fears are the roadblocks that will detour your journey."*

Step 3 Creating a Road Map

Your next step is creating a road map that follows your interests. Go back to your list of clues and pinpoint your most marketable talents. Then take a look at how you may take what you love and create your life path—your career. Any of these opportunities may be available to you based on your level of skill, knowledge, and work experience.

Not everything in your career is going to be fun. But you can make it fun. There will be times in your career that you will have to buckle down and work hard to gain new skills and insights about your craft. At times you may feel awkward or disinterested in what you are learning. You may even be tempted to avoid experiencing something new because you don't like it.

Just because you don't like doing something doesn't mean you have the option of not doing it. For example, you may not like to work out, but it's important to be in good shape so that you can look the part of a beauty professional. Instead of dreading exercise, go to the gym and find someone who is in better shape than you are and work out with that person.

Find people to play with while you learn and build your career. Choose to hang around with people who want to play with you. Little kids are brilliant at this. They focus their attention on other people who want to play with them. So don't waste your energy on professional friends who don't want to learn or experience what the industry has to offer. Follow the SW, SW, SW philosophy: Some will want to play. Some won't want to play. So what!

> *Follow the SW, SW, SW philosophy:*
>
> *Some will want to play. Some won't want to play. So what!"*

Connecting Tip #26

SW, SW, SW

Decide to make your career path fun. Find people who want to join you and who also want to have fun "playing with you," while building a career. Remember the SW, SW, SW philosophy.

Take Your First Step

 For most professionals entering the industry, your first step may include working with clients within a spa, salon, or retail store. Some states may allow you to be a student instructor or assistant to an instructor right out of school. Here are examples of entry-level opportunities:

Salon/Day Spa Positions

- Hair stylist
- Hair color specialist
- Skin care therapist
- Spa therapist
- Makeup artist
- Nail technician
- Massage therapist

Other Positions

- Student instructor
- Retail specialist
- Assistant freelance makeup artist or hair stylist for print, television, or film
- Distributor customer service or salon sales consultant
- Salon customer service
- Service desk representative

Most salons have training programs that may last from one month to a year or longer, depending on the level of expertise and skill required by the salon. Your initial salon training is extremely valuable and can set the tone for the remainder of your career. Take time to find a salon, spa, or school environment that is right for you. In **Step 4** you will receive additional information about salon positions. But before you focus on the different types of salon environments, let's look at the big picture of what your career could entail. These are the next steps you will take after you have gained some initial experience.

The following is a list of opportunities that are available to you after you have had some initial training and experience. The positions listed below all require specific skills and knowledge. On the left, you will notice a description of your potential interests or skills. On the right are career options.

CAREER OPPORTUNITIES

Training and Education

If you love to learn and coach others you may have a talent for these positions.

Salon Education Director — Create and lead staff training and development. Salon education directors are in charge of training new staff and mentoring experienced staff. The education director arranges the educational calendar and works with internal trainers and guest educators to facilitate in-salon training sessions.

School Instructor — Lead, motivate, and mentor Future Professionals. School instructor positions have become prestigious and financially rewarding.

Technical Educator — If you have a special technical interest or talent for haircutting, chemical reformation, or hair color, become a technical educator for one of the many professional product-manufacturing companies.

Sales and Service

If you love to promote products and serve others, here are some opportunities for you.

Retail Product Educator — Many product-manufacturing companies employ educators to train their network of Salon Professionals and school professionals. If product knowledge and retail sales come naturally to you, you may want to consider this position.

Retail Manager — The potential in product and retail sales within and outside of the industry is growing every year. Check out large salons that have focused retail store environments. Talk to your salon owner about expanding the salon retail space or pursue a product company that has opened a retail division.

Admissions Representative or Admissions Leader — Become a mentor to Future Professionals and help others attain their career goals. Attract Future and Salon Professionals to our industry by working in school admissions.

Salon Sales Consultant — Become a consultant to salons by working for a product or equipment distribution company. As a salon consultant you will have a territory of salons and schools. You must be self-directed and have great presentation, sales, and organization skills.

Spa Manager — The day and destination spa business continues to grow. Many hotels, resorts, and health clubs are expanding or opening spas to meet demand. Lead and direct a team of spa specialists.

Creative Trends

If you have a creative edge or flair for following and setting trends, you may be just the person for these positions.

Creative/Technical Director — Many large salon organizations have created a distinct company image. They may be interested in your ability to create seasonal looks to feature in their service menus, advertising, training programs, and print work.

Platform Artist — Let your creativity flow. Develop your stage presence and public speaking ability. Channel your creativity into educating and inspiring audiences in a variety of industry shows.

Sessions Stylist — This specialized field melds creativity and technical genius into art. Breaking into photo, television, video, or film work requires superior technical skill, a talent for predicting trends, and a passion for capturing the best image.

Leadership and Management

If you like to organize salon events or programs, here are some ideas.

Salon Management — After establishing yourself in a salon, you may want to ask your salon owner about becoming a salon team leader. Salon managers are responsible for the success of the salon operations. They hire and coach staff, as well as lead salon operations and system development.

School or Academy Director — Lead and coach a school team in developing curriculum, meeting enrollment goals, and coaching Future Professionals. This highly demanding job will provide you with many learning opportunities.

Distribution Sales Manager — Lead and manage salon sales consultants who place and promote retail and professional product lines within salons, spas, and schools. If you are highly motivated and organized, this is a position for you.

Show Coordinator — Many manufacturing companies have teams that organize education events and shows. The show coordinator's job requires organizational skills, flexibility, the ability to stay calm under pressure, and the freedom to travel extensively.

Entrepreneurship

If you have a passion for creating and leading your own business, here are some business ideas to consider.

Salon Boutique — Get your feet wet by opening a boutique salon. Start small and learn the basics of business by leasing a suite or working in a small, one to four-chair salon.

Salon/Spa — Open a salon or spa. Learn the business first by observing your boss. Ask for his or her help or interview other successful salon owners. You, too, can create a salon or spa empire like Robert Cromeans or David Wagner.

School — The school business is one of the best-kept secrets. Although the initial investment is substantial, the opportunities for personal and financial growth are great. If you truly have a passion for learning, become a school owner like Winn Claybaugh, co-founder of PAUL MITCHELL THE SCHOOL.

Product Company — Now this is thinking big! Entrepreneurial individuals like John Paul DeJoria founded many of today's successful product companies. He is the co-founder of John Paul Mitchell Systems. He and his partner, Paul Mitchell, started with a dream, then pursued their passion and achieved success.

Step 4 Making It Happen

Now that you are clear on what you want, let's discover how to make it happen. In this segment we will share several important suggestions that include shopping around for the right salon and career tips that will help you to create your career path.

Explore the Possibilities

Before you make a commitment to a company, make sure you have all of the facts. Do a little research on what is available to you. As you are gathering information, realize that during your research you can gain valuable contacts and make important first impressions with potential future employers. As you shop for where you want to be, remember you are also being evaluated for your potential. Make sure to dress and act as if you are going in for an interview. Make a great first impression.

CREATING YOUR CAREER
ROAD MAP

❶ Choose your path. Determine what you want from your profession.

❷ Make it fun. Find mentors and people to "play" with.

❸ Take your first step. Work in a salon or spa that will further your goals.

❹ Identify your next steps. Open up to possibilities and opportunities.

❺ Ask if you can hang out at the salon and observe. Here are some things you may want to consider in your research:

Look at the salon atmosphere and location — Observe the salon environment. Is it comfortable, clean, and service-friendly? Do you feel comfortable there?

Observe the salon image — Check out the salon advertising, printed materials, and Web site.

Connect with the salon owner/manager — Ask for an informational interview.

Talk with the salon team — Shadow team members for a couple of days and ask them to share their insights and experiences.

SUSIE

Susie Fields is the president of Salon Training International. Her focus is to support business owners, entrepreneurs, and sales professionals in building successful companies. She has helped salons become more systematic and successful. Salon Training International has a team of trainers that provides education in almost every area of the industry. Susie is a great example of how you may take your unique skills and create a career that you will love.

Have you ever had the thought, "What's next? Where do I go from here?" I considered these questions about five years ago. I was making an amazing income working behind the chair four days per week in the salon. I reached a place in my career where I wanted more challenge and wanted to make a difference in the industry. I wanted to do something new. I asked myself, "What are my career options?"

> "Have you ever had the thought, 'What next?'"

I started working as a part-time sales consultant with a distributor in San Diego. I realized that it was a great opportunity for me to be able to give back to the salon industry and to see how salons did business. I was able to see what worked for successful salons. I also had the opportunity to observe what was missing at the salons that were not doing so well. I noticed that a lot of stylists were waiting to build a clientele. I would see them in salons reading magazines and looking for clients between the pages, when actually the clients were right outside their doors. They just needed to go find them.

I started putting classes together for my salons and had a phenomenal response. My goal was to teach professionals how to build their businesses and in turn grow my own business. I found from my experience that I had a passion for speaking. I looked for opportunities to contribute and make that difference. During this time, I discovered the writings of Abraham Maslow, a psychologist, who believed that human beings go through different stages in their lives.

FIELDS

"The fourth stage is discovering that you want to be unique and to be recognized for the talent that you have."

The first stage is survival, where food, shelter, and clothing are the issues. The second stage is building security for tomorrow and gaining some stability in your life. The third stage is belonging. Everyone wants to belong, to be part of a team. The fourth stage is discovering that you want to be unique and to be recognized for the talent that you have. Maslow's theory stated that the highest level a person could attain as a human being was "self-actualization," meaning you know who you are and how to create what you want. When you reach the point of self-actualization and all your other needs are met, you then want to start contributing and making a difference in the world.

After several training sessions, people started asking, "Do you have a book? Do you have any tapes?" I began putting my notes together, and three years later published my book *Passion: A Salon Professional's Handbook to Building a Successful Business*. I hired a team of people to support me in marketing my speaking business and created a whole training and development business for the salon industry.

What I have discovered throughout my career is that when you come to a spiritual understanding of who you are, which is not necessarily a religious feeling but a deep feeling within your spirit, you can begin to take control of your life and destiny.

The Informational Interview

While in school you may want to start researching companies. Start by scheduling informational interviews. An informational interview involves meeting with a salon owner or manager to identify employment opportunities and to get information that will help you to make an informed career decision. Remember that as you interview potential employers, they are also evaluating your potential. This is your opportunity to make a great first impression.

INFORMATIONAL INTERVIEWS

1. **Be prepared with at least five questions.** Your questions may be about training, career opportunities, salon clientele, and team activities.

2. **Look the part of a successful professional.**

3. **Shake the salon owner's or manager's hand and thank the interviewer for his or her time.**

4. **Smile and be friendly.**

5. **If you are interested, ask for a formal interview.**

6. **Send a thank-you card.** See thank-you card ideas in this chapter.

Why would you want to interview potential employers, before they interview you? An informational interview can help you to gather important facts that may affect your decision to work at the salon. It's important to get firsthand information about the employer rather than relying on hearsay, when you are making career decisions.

You will also notice that there are many different types of salons and spas to choose from. It is important that you work in a salon that is compatible with your goals.

SALON OPPORTUNITIES

SALON TYPE	DESCRIPTION	ADVANTAGES
Boutique Salons	Small, one to four chairs. Owner probably manages the salon, is in charge of training, and services an established clientele.	Intimate environments and personalized mentoring. Informal work environments that may accommodate your unique approach to building your business.
Full Service Salons	Between five and 80 chairs. Offer a variety of services. May require completion of an extensive training program prior to working on your own clients. A manager may coach and direct the team.	Offer the opportunity to become part of a team. Option to offer a variety of services or work within a specialty department, like hair color or hair design departments.
Specialty Salons	Cater to a specific type of clientele offering special services to meet their needs. Examples are men's, hair color, or nail salons.	Designed to cater to a unique portion of the client market. Ideal for those with a special interest or technical talent.
Day Spas	Feature relaxing environments and services including facials, makeup services, massage, body treatments, and hand and foot services. May offer water treatments, saunas, steam rooms, and therapeutic whirlpool baths.	Wellness-oriented work environments broaden the beauty profession.
Value Salons	Feature high volume, cost-conscious service. Usually located in malls and other high volume retail areas. Offer quick, convenient services at cost-conscious prices.	Great training. Good places to gain experience. Busy atmosphere means fast business growth.
Chain Salons	May be privately owned or operated by large corporations.	Salons offer wonderful benefits, training, and opportunities to build a career. Many opportunities to grow as part of a large team.

Each salon environment is unique; therefore, it is important to find out about salons through visiting, rather than taking the word of your friends. Find the environment that is compatible with your work personality and where you can commit to working for at least five years.

Moving from salon to salon is not financially beneficial and is detrimental to building your clientele. It's best to do your homework up front, prior to accepting a position.

Prepare for Your New Role

Before you ever set foot in a salon it is important that you know something about the job that you are applying for. Most positions can be broken down into the following skill areas:

- **Knowledge** — The knowledge needed to perform successfully.

- **Attitude and attributes** — The personal characteristics and attitudes needed for success.

- **Behavior** — The skills and behavior needed to build your business.

What are the skills and knowledge of successful business people? What characteristics, attitudes, and beliefs do they have? How do they look and act? Your new position will require you to be knowledgeable, positive, and focused on success. The following self-checklist may be used to prepare for your new role. Check the statements you feel you have achieved and circle the ones that you feel you need to work on.

" Moving from salon to salon is not financially beneficial and is detrimental to building your clientele. It's best to do your homework up front, prior to accepting a position."

WHAT MAKES A PROFESSIONAL?

KNOWLEDGE	ATTITUDE AND ATTRIBUTES	BEHAVIOR
What knowledge do you already have?	What attitudes and attributes of success do you possess?	How must you behave to be successful?

KNOWLEDGE

What knowledge do you already have?

- Mastery of basic technical skills

- Great communication skills (verbal and nonverbal)

- Listening skills and the intent to understand and help others

- Enough knowledge to consult and provide recommendations and follow up with clients

- Excellent knowledge of products and services

- Knowledge of the industry and the salon you work for

- Knowledge of fashion and ability to talk about trends

- Knowledge of a variety of topics and well-read

ATTITUDE AND ATTRIBUTES

What attitudes and attributes of success do you possess?

- Enthusiastic and positive

- Enjoy helping others

- Take pride in what you do

- Look the part of a beauty professional

- Team player

- Positive and solution-oriented

- Service-oriented and flexible

- A good role model and lead by example

- Have integrity

- A lifelong learner and committed to self-development

- Self-disciplined

BEHAVIOR

How must you behave to be successful?

- Self-motivated to build your business as though you are self-employed

- On time or arrive early

- Do what it takes to get the job done and stay late if needed

- Keep your work area clean and pitch in as needed

- Mentor and coach others

- Pursue new trends and creative techniques

- Support company guidelines

- Maintain retail and service goals

- Look the part of a successful image professional and consultant

- Provide consistent, quality services

- Continually focus and build your business through referrals, recruiting, retailing, rebooking, and retention

Beginning Your Job Search

There are three tools you will need to promote yourself during the interview process: a résumé, an introductory letter, and a thank-you card.

Chapter 4 provided a guide to résumés and cover letters. It is important to keep these materials up-to-date at all times as opportunities may pop up at a moment's notice. You will want to be prepared to take advantage of all opportunities to promote yourself.

Once your résumé and cover letter are written, and you have decided which of the salons you have visited match your career goals, begin networking. Call the salons that you visited and completed informational interviews with. Talk to the manager and remind him or her of your visit. Get employment leads at shows, education events, and industry gatherings. Review the employment opportunity board or files at your school.

The interview is your opportunity to determine if the school or team is right for you, so ask a lot of questions."

The Formal or Technical Interview

The interview process is the time that a potential employer is assessing your skill level, confidence, and knowledge. He or she is also trying to determine if your personality and talents will fit into the existing salon team. Most importantly, he or she is evaluating how you will service and support the salon clients. It is important for you to be prepared, focused, and relaxed. Employers know that this process is a little nerve-racking and will expect you to be a little nervous. The best way to combat nervousness is to be overly prepared. The interview is your opportunity to determine if the school or team is right for you, so ask a lot of questions.

PREPARING FOR A JOB
INTERVIEW

❶ Purchase two complete outfits that reflect your personal style. Go back to **Chapter 2** for tips on what to wear.

❷ Make sure your hair is cut and colored to reflect the most up-to-date trends. On the day of your interview, style your hair and do your makeup and nails.

❸ Bring an extra copy of your résumé. You may also want to bring a list of your references, list of seminars and accomplishments, and photos of your work.

❹ Find at least two to three different models who can be available for your technical interview. Choose models with beautiful hair that is easy to work with. This is not a time to tackle a challenging head of hair.

Prior to the technical interview, make sure your model's hair is colored and makeup is done. Have your model wear something very simple, like a black dress or outfit. Always have a back-up model, just in case the one you selected cannot make the appointment.

THE FORMAL JOB INTERVIEW

1. Breathe and relax your body.

2. Shake the interviewer's hand and smile.

3. Be friendly and confident.

4. Answer questions completely and confidently. See interview questions for ideas.

5. Share your goals and provide an overview explanation of your résumé.

6. Ask questions about the training programs, compensation, responsibilities, team meetings, salon events, and activities.

7. Ask about the hiring process, company benefits, and your next steps to gaining employment.

8. Thank the interviewer for his or her time.

9. Make sure your body language is professional and relaxed. Smile, shake hands, stand and sit using good posture, and maintain eye contact with the interviewer.

10. Before leaving get the mailing address. Always send a thank-you note within 24 hours.

THE TECHNICAL JOB INTERVIEW

1. Bring all of the tools and products you will use.

2. Make sure your equipment is clean and organized.

3. Set up your station.

4. Do a complete consultation.

5. Tell the interviewer what you plan to do with the client.

6. Do a scalp massage. Shampoo your client. Make sure to clean the shampoo area before returning to your station.

7. Perform the service professionally. Use clean partings and a systematic approach.

8. Ask the interviewer if she would like to check your work prior to styling.

9. Complete the style. This is the most important part! Make your model look beautiful.

10. Recommend home care to your model and touch up her makeup if necessary.

11. Sweep up and clean your station.

Interview Q&A

Here are examples of questions your interviewer may ask:

Interviewer: **Why don't you start out and tell me a little about yourself.**

You: *Briefly share personal and professional information about yourself. Outline your school and past work experience.*

Interviewer: **What accomplishments are you most proud of?**

You: *Briefly share accomplishments, activities, and seminars you have attended.*

Interviewer: **Why should I hire you?**

You: *Share your most important characteristics and what you think you can contribute.*

Interviewer: **What are some of your career goals?**

You: *Be prepared with a couple of ideas on where you want to go in the future.*

Interviewer: **What do you feel you need to learn or what skills do you think you need to develop?**

You: *Mention areas where you need improvement and growth. Share them honestly.*

Be prepared with several questions about the position you are applying for. Ask questions to uncover information about the salon training program, types of education and training available outside of the salon, compensation, company career opportunities, job description, and clientele or service procedures.

Be confident and relaxed during the interview. You want to show that you have the ability to communicate and work well under pressure. Take time to thank your interviewer and arrange a follow-up. End the meeting with a handshake and a time or date for a follow-up call.

Thank-You Cards

Send a thank-you card within 24 hours following your interview. It should be personal and hand-written. Even if you don't receive a job offer or have decided to pursue other employers, you still want to send a thank-you note. It reflects your good manners.

- Thank the interviewers for their time.
- Compliment their businesses.
- State how you will follow up with a phone call.

Also remember that the beauty and salon industry is very small. This interviewer may not offer you a position, but if you impressed her, she may refer you to someone else. Employers love nice people. If you connect with them during the interview, they will want to help you. Never burn any bridges, no matter what your interview experience was like. Always follow up with a thank-you note.

THANK-YOU NOTES ARE:
- **Hand-written**
- **Mailed the next day**
- **A show of gratitude**

THANK-YOU NOTES ARE NOT:
- **E-mails**
- **Mailed weeks later**
- **A place to plead your case**

March 1, 2004

Dear Ms. Winters:

I would sincerely like to thank you for the wonderful opportunity to visit your salon and spend time with you and Jennifer Johnson. You have a beautiful salon and an excellent business. I learned a great deal from our conversation.

I look forward to hearing more about the opportunities your company has to offer. Thank you for your time.

Sincerely,
Pamela Miller

Interview Follow-up

After the interview is complete, be confident and assured that you did the best you could do. Follow up with a call, if you did not hear back from the potential employer in the time you were given. Finally, if your interviews do not generate a job offer, quickly move on. Continue to look until you have exactly the position in the salon or company that you want. Don't get stuck waiting for one company to hire you; stay open to all of your options.

Be persistent — Your target company may not have a current opening, but there are hundreds of companies who need new talent. You just have to find them. You may not get your dream job in the time frame you wanted, but if you persist, you eventually will attain your dreams.

Reinvent yourself — As you create your career path, you may discover that your dream employer is your present one. The company or salon you are working for may have additional opportunities for growth. Work with your salon owner or manager to reinvent your position by getting involved in education, shows, salon events, or mentoring. Continually reinvent what you do and how you do it. You will be surprised at how fascinating your career can be.

Step 5 Follow Your Heart

Our final step on our journey to connecting to your future is following your heart. This simply means being clear on what makes your heart sing. What do you love to do? What career do you want to create? Who do you love doing it with?

What type of people do you want to work with? What type of clientele do you want to attract and develop long-term relationships with? Following your heart means you are clear on what you want and you honor the things that make you happy.

MICHAEL

Michael Cole's track record in the salon industry has been absolutely phenomenal. He has accumulated over 30 years of experience as a stylist, manager, executive chain director, and multiple salon location owner. For the last 20 years Michael has been the founder and president of Salon Development Corporation, an international company specializing in salon business training. The key to Michael's success is his unique ability to observe current and future trends and translate them into methods by which salons achieve growth.

Earn a living or design a life? Your career can provide you with a comfortable income, but it can also provide you financial abundance and a lifestyle of your dreams.

You can create what you want by simply focusing your thoughts. "Intention" is defined as focusing your attention on a specific task until it is complete. The *principle of conscious intention* means that you are deliberately focusing your attention, without being distracted, until you meet your goals. Your intentions are very powerful. Whatever you focus on will eventually happen.

Make a conscious decision to focus your thoughts, starting now. If you are currently working, think about where you focus your attention during your work hours. Do you just go through the motions and allow things to come to you? Or do you consciously focus your attention on the results you want to achieve? The majority of people simply wait for things to happen. They don't take the initiative to create success. I call them the *natural growers.*

A *natural grower* is someone in the 80 percent-majority who is happy simply accommodating and serving their clients.

They experience natural growth through price increases and additional clientele. They serve their clients and may provide a product recommendation if asked. They wait for the client to initiate additional services and product purchases.

COLE

Natural growers don't want to step out of the box and perform beyond the norm. They make an average income and they experience a gradual and slow growth.

The top 20 percent are those I call the *self-initiated growers*. They put the principle of conscious intention into action. They recognize that they are the source of their growth and consistently set into action the things that bring them phenomenal success. They are always looking for ways to create rapid growth.

You have the ability to make $80,000 to $100,000 a year, if you consciously focus your attention on the things that create financial success. Here are a few suggestions to help to self-initiate your growth.

> "You have the ability to make $80,000 to $100,000 a year, if you consciously focus your attention on the things that create financial success."

- Grow beyond busy by focusing your attention on the 4 R's: retail, rebooking, referrals, and recommendations.

- Keep your eyes off the disbelievers and find self-initiated growers to hang out with and learn from.

- Consciously make decisions about your business every moment you are with your clients.

- Create synergy by finding others who think like you and spend time with them consciously initiating growth.

- Finally, don't wait to understand to take action. Just do it! Through your actions you will learn how to design your life.

THE 4 R'S TO
PROFESSIONAL SUCCESS

① **Retail** – Recommend retail products to every client. Don't wait for your client to ask. Make suggestions throughout the service. Complete each service by sharing your final product suggestions when you know your client is happy with her service.

② **Recommendations** – It's not what's on your book, it's what you do with your book that counts. Recommend add-on services to each of your clients during every service. Squeeze services in.

Suggest color fresheners, texture services, makeup services, and eyebrow shaping. Recommend and do whatever it takes to recommend services to the max.

③ **Rescheduling** – Always rebook your clients before they leave. Don't wait for them to initiate the next service appointments. Schedule their next appointments and focus on booking additional services. Rebooking is one of the most important things you can do to retain your clients.

④ **Referrals** – Ask your loyal and satisfied clients to refer their friends and family. Give them business cards and thank them when they support you.

THE 4 R'S

1. Retail

2. Recommendations

3. Rescheduling

4. Referrals

Connecting Tip   #27

Your Success Is Guaranteed!

There is no way you can fail. You will discover that each experience is a lesson and that you have control over your journey. Remember to:

Step 1 Get clear.
Step 2 Let go.
Step 3 Create a road map.
Step 4 Make it happen.
Step 5 Follow your heart.

MY GAME PLAN

PLAN
In this chapter you learned about the many opportunities in the beauty profession. The last step of your game plan is to map your career path. Make a commitment to develop your future. **Write your commitment here.**

REFLECT
Think about what fears or obstacles may interfere with keeping your commitment. **Write them here.**

TAKE ACTION

CLARIFY
Clarify what you want. Do you want a career or a job? Identify your interests and talents. Visualize your future.

LET GO
Clear the roadblocks in your mind. Let go of fear. Create an affirmation. Focus on your goals.

CHOOSE
Choose a path. Make it fun.

VISUALIZE
See the big picture. Be informed about industry opportunities. Determine which environment best fits you.

PREPARE
Prepare for your new role. Identify your strengths and areas to develop. Create a job-hunting plan.

FINAL CURTAIN CALL

So, do you feel like you're ready to conquer the world? Do you feel as though anything is possible for you in the industry of beauty? Money? Fame? Adventure? Travel? Making a difference? If so, you're completely right! This industry is unlimited in its opportunities, and even more unlimited in the number of people who want to help you realize your dreams.

This is an industry based on your DESIRE. Perhaps your haircutting abilities are not what you want them to be. Perhaps your verbal skills need some polishing, or maybe your customer service skills need work. All of that's okay because here and now you can show up with the one thing that will take you further than the skills defined in some of the chapters of this book. That is DESIRE! If you show up with desire, doors will open up for you.

I have had people approach me for a job who had a résumé worth admiring. They had the education, experience, technical talent, but they were missing a spark. On the other hand, I have had people come to me without any experience or résumé but who possessed tons of desire with an attitude of "I know I can do it. Just give me the chance!" That's the type of person that I want to hire.

What does desire look like? That's easy! You are the first to arrive and the last to leave. You show up with an attitude of, "What's in it for us today?" You let everyone know that you are available for anything and everything. Yes, you'll fold towels. Yes, you'll sweep up everyone's hair. Yes, you'll clean the rest rooms 20 times a day if necessary. Yes, you are always in a great mood, and faking it on the days when you're not. Yes, you are available for mentoring, schooling, coaching, and guiding.

Go ahead and fine-tune your technical abilities. Upgrade your image. Keep showing up for every class, seminar, and show you can find. But while you're doing all of that, always, always let the people around you know — both through your words and your actions — that you have the desire to be a passionate, loving, dedicated Salon Professional. Enjoy the journey. I certainly have.

Winn Claybaugh
PAUL MITCHELL THE SCHOOL

Sources

Callahan, Tommy. *The Learning System.* JOHN PAUL MITCHELL SYSTEMS, 1995.

McCarthy, Bernice. *4Mat System.* EXCEL, Inc., 1980.

Papageorgio, Susan. *Game Planning Curriculum.* Inspired Learning LLC, 1997.

Vannoy, Steven W. *Ten Greatest Gifts I Give My Children: Parenting from the Heart.* Simon and Schuster, 1994.

PAUL MITCHELL THE SCHOOL Publications

Core Cutting DVD Box Set
3-DVD box set that includes an interactive visual learning library featuring nine haircut exercises.

Core Cutting Guide
A study guide with detailed technical explanations and step-by-step procedures.

Core Cutting Leader's Guide
Trainer's workbook featuring curriculum and interactive lesson plans, curriculum outlines, and skill check forms.

Core Cutting Product Recipe Cards and Skill Cards
Technical quick-reference tools designed to enhance learning on the clinic floor or salon service area.

Core Cutting Diagramming System Portfolio
A unique mapping tool and diagramming key designed to improve haircut-blueprinting skills.

Core Cutting Diagramming Pads
Additional 50-sheet diagramming head form pads.

Core Cutting Diagramming Stencils
3-Large head diagram stencils used to create classroom visuals.

Program Holder
Organize your curriculum materials in a sleek PAUL MITCHELL THE SCHOOL document file.

Connecting To My Future
A learning and planning guide for Salon Professionals. (8-CD Audio Book)

Connecting To My Future
A learning and planning guide for Salon Professionals. (190 page book)

Attracting The Future
A guide for schools and salons to recruit future Salon Professionals.
(200 page book)

10 Opportunities and 2-Minute Plan
Quick reference cards, pack of 50.

Be Nice (Or Else!)
And what's in it for you... (194 page book)

Place your order today!
Call **1-866-302-5576** toll-free or visit
www.PAULMITCHELLTHESCHOOL.com.
Checks, VISA, and MasterCard accepted.